STANDING FOR YOUR MARRIAGE GOD'S WAY

Do You Trust God to Restore Your Relationship?

Simone Middlebrooks

Copyright © [2024]

Simone Middlebrooks

All rights reserved.

The content of this book is the intellectual property of Simone Middlebrooks, therefore, no part of this book may be reproduced, distributed, or transmitted in any form or by any means, including photocopying, recording, or other electronic or mechanical methods, without the prior written permission of the author, except in the case of brief quotations embodied in critical reviews and certain other non-commercial uses permitted by copyright law.

For permission contact: divinepurposepartner@gmail.com

& divinepurposepartner.com

First Edition: 2024

Dedication

I dedicate this book to my late father, who passed away in 2011, and my spiritual father, who passed away in 2024. Both of them had a big impact on my life. My spiritual father often reminded me of Proverbs 3:5-6: *"Trust in the Lord with all your heart and lean not on your own understanding; in all your ways acknowledge Him, and He will direct your path."*

Table of Contents

Introduction

The subject of marriage is so critical to not only the family structure, but to the society at large. You will also agree with me that societal breakdown of law and order is sometimes traced to the failure in our family structures, which is ultimately a result of failed marriages.

These days, the virus of divorce does not only plague marriages of unbelievers, but also Christians. In fact, the rate of divorce among Christians is also alarming. The question is, why? Why do we have believers fail in their second or even third marriages? Why is it so difficult to see couples celebrate 40 to 50 years of blissful marriage? Don't you think something is off somewhere?

To continue this introduction, I will like to highlight a few statistics on divorce publishes by Forbes. Research from sources such as the U.S. Census, the CDC, Pew Research, and others was combined to explore the factors contributing to divorce in the United States. I know you're excited to see it. Let's take a look!

In 2022, there were 673,989 divorces and annulments recorded across 45 U.S. states that report this data. During the same year, 2,065,905 marriages took place, with the national marriage rate at 6.2 per 1,000 people.

The common claim that half of all marriages end in divorce is not entirely accurate, at least for first marriages. Only 43% of first marriages result in divorce. Buy hey, isn't that too much? Now, the likelihood of divorce increases with subsequent marriages, with 60% of second marriage. In fact, for third marriages, it's up to 70%.

They striking issues here is that, many of these divorce cases are between two believers in Christ. Again, I ask, why? Was that the original plan of God for marriages when He was instituting it in Genesis chapter one? Why are people not defending this great institution anymore? Why can't we stand for our marriages?

This book is for those who are standing for their marriage. Your spouse may have left, walked out the door, and is now with someone else, and you're asking God to restore your marriage. Before we go any further, I need to ask: did God put you two together? Think long and hard about this. Was God involved in your dating, engagement, and marriage? If the answer is no, we have a bigger problem than just the current situation. I'm not saying it can't be resolved or that God can't fix it, but you're asking God to restore something that He was never in from the beginning.

Here's what you're doing: "Hey God, it's me again. My spouse left, and I really want them back in our home. How do I go about this? I need help." And God might be looking at you like, "You're asking me to fix something I wasn't invited into from the start." He can fix it, but it's going to take work. Are you going to trust Him fully in this process to fix your marriage? You'll probably say, "Yes, Lord, I'm going to trust you wholeheartedly, without doubt."

But here's the problem: the enemy will attack your heart, mind, body, and soul. He will make you believe God isn't working, and you'll start to doubt. Let me be real with you—this will delay the process because every time you doubt, you cancel out what God is trying to do for you. James 1:6-7 supports this: "But ask in faith, never doubting, for the one who doubts is like a wave of the sea, driven and tossed by the wind. For the doubter, being double-minded and unstable in every way, must not expect to receive anything from the Lord."

The proof is right there. I'm not saying this journey will be easy. I'm not saying you can't get through it or that God can't do the impossible, but it will take work—especially if God didn't put you together in the first place. This is going to be a faith walk. Every time doubt tries to creep in and question what God has told you, ask Him to help your unbelief because you'll need it.

So, your spouse has left, and you're missing them. You hear they're with someone else, and that's like a dagger to your heart. Don't lie to yourself because I know how it feels when this happens. You start asking yourself, "How did I let this happen?" You get all these things swirling in your head, and then you start doubting that God is the author and finisher of your faith. This is where you must stop yourself before sinking into a dark place and start believing the enemy's lies. I don't care what you see or hear; your focus must be on God and God alone.

If you want God to restore your marriage, the first thing you need to do is ask Him to deal with you. Yes, you might say, "I didn't do anything wrong; I didn't cause this mess." But it takes two. Sorry, reality check—it doesn't take just one person to create problems in a marriage. You played a part, and so did your spouse.

You need to go to God and ask, "Lord, search my heart. Show me what I did to contribute to the separation between myself and my spouse. Show me myself—don't show me my husband or wife. Show me, because I need to deal with myself first." In the next few pages, there's space for you to write down everything you think you contributed to the breakdown. This is a self-evaluation—just you, not your spouse.

Once you've done this self-evaluation, start praying for yourself. Deal with your issues. Get down to the nitty-gritty. I've provided two prayers: one for those who didn't include God in the beginning of their relationship and marriage, and one for those who did.

Your journey to stand for your marriage starts with seeking God's guidance, praying for yourself and your spouse, fasting, and trusting Him to do the work in His time. Stay strong, stay faithful, and above all, stay connected to God.

As you read this book, I earnestly pray that God will help to stand for your marriage. For those who are almost giving up, the Lord will encourage, and strengthen you to fight till the end in the name of Jesus. Enjoy the reading.

Chapter 1

Who Or What Is The Foundation Of Your Marriage?

Becky met Anderson in a grocery store; they exchanged phone contact numbers, and went out on few occasions. Thereafter, Anderson asked Becky to move in with him. Becky, knowing fully well that Bible frowns at co-existing without any form of legal backing is fornication, still yielded out of desperation.

After living together for about 2 years, and a baby added to them, they decided to get married. Six months after formalizing their union, issues came up, and Anderson decided to file for a divorce. Becky thought it was a joke until she received the divorce papers. Couldn't they have resolved their differences? Or, what do you think? Something seems wrong here, isn't it?

The scripture says, "If the foundation be destroyed, what can the righteous do?" Like I often say, there's something the righteous can do – pray!

Truth is, the foundation of everything we do on earth matters. The quality, and depth of the foundation of a house determines its strength and durability. Buildings last long based on the foundations upon which they are built. Marriages collapse like buildings due to faulty foundations. If you're reading this book, and you're not married yet congratulations. Please take time to build a strong, and formidable foundation for an ideal Christian marriage.

While I meditate on the case of Becky and Anderson, I realize their foundation was totally wrong. In the same report shared by Forbes, it was discovered that research from 2018 found that while couples who live together before marriage may face a reduced risk of divorce in the first year of marriage, the likelihood of divorce increases in the years that follow. ***Specifically, 34% of those who cohabited before engagement experienced divorce***, compared to 22% of couples who waited until after engagement or marriage to live together.

Beloved, you can clearly see here that even academic research shows that co-habitation before marriage could also lead to divorce. Truth is, what's there to look up to on the wedding night, if a man has seen a woman so cheaply before they are lawfully joined?

Now, before I continue, I will like to establish the fact that quite a good number of married women, or even men, don't know why they are married. And like they say, "If the purpose of a thing isn't known, abuse is certainly inevitable. To continue in this chapter, I will take time define marriage, explain the concept of an ideal foundation for Christian marriage, and how to fix faulty foundation.

What is Marriage?

Marriage, as an institution, holds a foundational and irreplaceable place in human society. Established by God before the fall of Adam and Eve, it reflects profound spiritual realities. Among these, marriage symbolizes the relationship between God and His people, pointing forward to the ultimate union between Christ and His Church at the culmination of history.

It is also looked at as a sacred covenant in which one man and one woman, free from any conditions that would invalidate their union, enter into a lifelong commitment. Both parties must be fully aware of all relevant matters before exchanging solemn vows in a public ceremony. In this covenant, they agree to fulfill all marital responsibilities, including a bond of exclusive sexual fidelity, for the duration of their shared lives. The marriage is consummated through sexual union, further sealing their commitment. So, you see from this definition that God instituted marriage.

Is God the Foundation of Your Marriage?

A Nigerian girl Tosin shared how she got married, and never peace in her home. Herself and her husband weren't fully saved at the time they got married. Although, Tosin had a form of godliness but never really committed to biblical teachings. Their marriage became threatened, and was tending towards divorce; nobody wanted to listen to the other. They fought on a regular basis. At a point, it was more like two enemies living together. According to her, divorce was really staring at her.

It was at this junction she decided to rededicate herself to Jesus. To her surprise, God took control within short time. Her husband also surrendered his life to Christ, and peace returned. Beloved, you need Jesus to be the Chief Corner Stone of your marriage.

You've probably heard of or seen people celebrating their 50th wedding anniversaries, right? We often wonder what the secret to their lasting union is—what has kept them together all these years. The answer is not far-fetched. Every couple must have the right foundation and live by the right principles, both in their words and actions. Unfortunately, many marriages today reach a point wherethe husband and wife become weary of one another and eventually part ways. However, God's desire is for marriages to be strong and enduring. He wants them to last and be rooted in the right foundation, upheld by the right values.

The most important foundation for a strong marriage is a relationship with the Lord. As Psalm 127:1 state, "Unless the Lord builds the house, the builders labor in vain." A lasting, strong marriage must be grounded in God and His guidance. Without Him, the efforts put into building a marriage will not reach their full potential.

Are You Married to Jesus?

As believers, we are called to understand that God desires a deep, covenantal relationship with us, both as His collective body and individually as His children. This relationship is grounded in His love for us, demonstrated through the sacrifice of Jesus Christ on the cross. The depth of His love is beyond comprehension, as He endured unimaginable suffering to draw us into a personal union with Him.

This divine relationship isn't a distant or symbolic one—it is intimate, personal, and eternal. At the point of our salvation, when we accept Christ as our Savior, we enter into a binding spiritual covenant with God. This covenant is similar to marriage, where we commit our lives to Him, and He, in turn, commits to us with a love that will never be separated by any power or force (Romans 8:38-39).

Every true Christian is Spiritually married to Christ; yes! But there shall be final marriage with the lamb at the return of the Son of God. The Apostle Paul, in Ephesians 5:21-32, draws a direct parallel between the union of a husband and wife and the relationship between Christ and His Church. Here, Paul teaches that the mystery of marriage on earth is a reflection of the greater spiritual union we are destined for with Christ. Truth is, you can't have this knowledge and miss it in marriage. In fact, every man or woman, who knows that Jesus is coming back for the church, will definitely be careful in handling his/her marriage.

"For this reason, a man shall leave his father and mother and be united to his wife, and the two shall become one flesh. This is a profound mystery—but I am talking about Christ and the Church" (Ephesians 5:31-32).

Paul points to the fact that marriage on earth symbolizes a far greater truth. Just as husband and wife are united, Christ unites with His Church—meaning that each believer is invited into an intimate, unbreakable relationship with the Savior. The question is, are you truly saved, and connected intimately with Christ? Are you truly married to

Jesus? A knowledge of this guarantees you a blissful marriage on earth.

This spiritual union between Christ and believers, often referred to as a "mystical marriage," is not about physical intimacy but spiritual oneness. This concept runs through scripture, highlighting how the earthly institution of marriage reflects a divine reality. Throughout history, Christian thinkers have seen this parallel in scripture—our relationship with Christ is like a marriage, one that transcends earthly limitations and brings us into a deep, eternal connection with God.

The reality of this spiritual union explains why Satan attacks the institution of marriage and the concept of sexual purity so fiercely. Marriage, designed by God, serves as a mirror of His relationship with humanity. When human marriage is corrupted or misunderstood, it distorts the image of the heavenly marriage between Christ and His people. By attacking marriage and sexuality, Satan aims to undermine our understanding of the divine union we are called into with God.

Our spiritual journey as Christians is, in many ways, preparing us for this eternal union with Christ. Just as marriage involves deep commitment, self-sacrifice, and unity, our relationship with Christ involves a transformation of our hearts and minds to reflect His image (Romans 8:29). Over time, we are conformed to His likeness, and this union deepens, ultimately culminating in the fullness of this union in eternity (1 John 3:2).

Why do I have to dig deep on this? Reason is, the depth of your union with God determines the depth of the foundation of your marriage. As believers, we are called to live with the awareness that we are already in a covenantal relationship with God. Just as a marriage requires dedication and fidelity, so too does our relationship with Christ. We must guard our hearts, pursue holiness, and live in purity, knowing that our lives are not our own but belong to the One who loved us and gave Himself for us.

"For your Maker is your husband—the Lord Almighty is his name" (Isaiah 54:5).

This profound truth shapes how we live, how we love, and how we relate to God and others. In our relationships on earth, especially in marriage, we reflect this divine love and unity, pointing to the ultimate fulfillment of God's plan—to be one with His people for all eternity. Allow this truth to help you win the battles of your marriage.

Now you can see God's original intention for marriage. Anything short of this model will always result in marital crisis. No doubt you can see where the real issues are — "THE FOUNDATION OF OUR MARRIAGE". But, is there hope for those with a wrong foundation? YES!

Mending the Faulty Foundation

To begin this part, I will love to congratulate those whose marriages are under satanic attack due to a faulty foundation. Yes! God is at work. The great restorer is about to do something remarkable in your marriage. Hallelujah!!!

Here's the good news;

Joel 2:25 says, "I will restore to you the years that the swarming locust has eaten, the hopper, the destroyer, and the cutter, my great army, which I sent among you." This verse communicates God's in infallible promise to heal, renew, and redeem what has been lost or broken, even after a season of hardship.

Applying this to a broken marriage offers hope, focusing on God's power to rebuild and renew relationships that have endured significant challenges.

Here a few things to learn from Joel 2:25. These few lessons will really help you a great deal as you trust God to mend the foundation of your marriage.

1. Commit to God's Promise of Restoration with Faith

In Joel 2:25, God promises to restore what has been lost. This same principle applies to a struggling marriage, where God's power can bring healing, even when damage seems beyond repair. Both partners can choose to have faith in God's ability to restore their marriage. Praying together and individually, ask God to bring back love, trust, and joy that may have diminished through past hurts or misunderstandings.

2. Acknowledge the Need for Repentance and Humility

The people of Israel were called to repentance before receiving the promise of restoration. Acknowledging faults and taking responsibility is crucial for healing. Each spouse should reflect on their role in the difficulties and be willing to seek forgiveness from both God and each other. This act of repentance allows God's healing to flow into the relationship, preparing the way for restoration.

3. Turn your Pain into Purpose

The difficult times Israel experienced became meaningful as they led to God's blessings. Likewise, God can bring purpose out of the pain in marriage. Instead of focusing on past mistakes, seek to understand how these experiences can strengthen the relationship. Ask what God wants you both to learn and how these lessons can make the marriage stronger and healthier.

4. Rebuild with Patience and Intention

God's promise of restoration implies a process, not an instant fix. Healing takes time and effort. Rebuilding requires steady commitment through loving actions and consistent trust-building efforts. Make time for each other, communicate openly, and support one another as you create new, positive experiences in your marriage, trusting God to work through each step.

5. Rely on God's Grace for Joy and Peace

God's promise of abundance and joy after a season of loss is a reminder that His grace can bring new happiness into marriage. Actively pray for God to fill your marriage with peace and joy. Replace negative thoughts with positive affirmations, gratitude, and encouragement for one another. Trust that God's grace can renew love in ways that go beyond previous experiences.

6. Seek Guidance from Christian Counsel and Community

God often provides support through community, and the wisdom of others can help sustain and restore marriage. Engage with a pastor, Christian counselor, or trusted friends who can encourage you along the way. They can offer advice, prayer, and accountability, helping both partners focus on the process of restoration.

7. Anticipate a New Season of Blessing and Unity

The passage also promises joy, abundance, and awareness of God's presence. This speaks to a fresh start in our marriages that brings greater blessings than before. Trust that God can lead you into a season of greater unity, love, and intimacy in your marriage. Bless and speak positively over your relationship, envision a hopeful future, and celebrate each small success, knowing that God is at work restoring what was lost.

Joel 2:25 reminds us that God can restore even the most damaged situations in marriages. For marriage, this involves faith, repentance, patience, and an ongoing commitment to healing. Embracing God's promises, practicing forgiveness, and nurturing spiritual growth together allows a couple to see their relationship flourish, showcasing God's ability to redeem and strengthen their bond beyond what they may have thought possible.

Wow! God is indeed a merciful God. There's hope for your marriage belove. The Lord will put things right in your marriage in the name of Jesus. Don't give up because you got it wrong from the foundation. The Master Builder is still in the business stabilizing faulty foundation. All you need do is cry to Him, and have faith in His unchanging power. And talking about "FAITH", you need enough of it to navigate this journey. Let's talk more about faith in the next chapter.

God bless you!

Prayer Points

Heavenly Father, thank You for making me come across this book.

Lord, I come to you just as I am. Have mercy on me for the areas I got it wrong in my marriage. Have mercy on my husband as well, and my marriage at large. Forgive us of every known and unknown errors.

My great restorer, I pray you will help to stabilize the foundation of my marriage in the name of Jesus. Help us to make You the only pivotal on which my marriage is hinged. Let the Holy Spirit take the center stage in my marriage in the name Jesus. Amen!

Chapter 2

Faith Vs. Doubt

elcome to this chapter as we look at the subject of Faith in combating the demon behind broken homes. Like we saw in the previous chapter, faith is very essential to mending faulty foundations of marriage. In fact, the subject of faith forms the basis for winner marital battles. We shall know more in a while.

Have you ever felt a quiet thread of doubt unraveling at the fabric of your marriage? Or perhaps, you've sensed the unshakable power of faith steadying your path? Great question, right? Truth is, doubt and faith often exist side by side in a Christian marriage, shaping how a couple grows together and confronts life's inevitable challenges. Whether you like it or not, the question will always be; "does doubt cloud your way further, or does faith become the anchor through life's storms?" While unchecked doubt can erode the foundation of a marriage, faith has the power to transform it into a rock-solid base of hope and unity. Looking at the interplay of faith and doubt, we uncover ways for couples to embrace faith in moments of uncertainty, creating a strong, spiritually fulfilled marriage.

At the heart of Christian marriage is the profound love Christ has for His Church—a sacred connection that, in the eyes of faith, calls couples to love each other with the same steadfastness. Yet, even within the context of a Christian marriage, doubt can arise. Doubts about a spouse, the direction of the relationship, or even faith itself may quietly seep in, especially during times of struggle. How couples navigate these moments can deeply impact the strength and resilience of their marriage. In this chapter we will examine the meaning of faith within marriage, how doubt manifests, and how couples can balance these forces to nurture a lasting bond, restore collapse relationships.

Marriage mirrors the covenant between God and His people, a sacred bond bound by trust and faith. Faith signifies not only trust in one's spouse but in God's divine design for marriage as well.

Faith: Trusting in God's Design

From a Christian perspective, marriage is intended for companionship, family, and a nurturing ground for faith.

Faith in marriage means believing that God's hand brought this union together and sustains it. Ephesians 5:31-33 illustrates this divine dimension, describing marriage as a mystery where two individuals become one—a holy covenant meant to reflect God's unwavering love. Couples who share this belief view their relationship as more than a legal bond; it's a divine calling.

Faith: Trusting in One Another

Faith within marriage also requires deep trust in each other. This trust, built on love, communication, and shared values, is not blind; it mirrors Christ's sacrificial love for the Church (Ephesians 5:25). Each partner trusts that the other has their best interests at heart and commits to supporting each other's spiritual, emotional, and physical well-being.

Faith: A Shared Spiritual Journey

In Christian marriage, faith is a journey taken together, creating a spiritual bond that fortifies the relationship. Couples who pray, worship, and share in life's experiences cultivate a faith that stands as a shield against life's hardships. This shared faith is a source of resilience, as both partners lean on God and each other to weather both joy and sorrow.

Yet, despite faith's significance, even the most devout Christian couples encounter doubt. Doubt is a natural part of human experience, and in marriage, it may arise in several ways.

When Doubt Enters the Marriage

Doubt in a Partner

Doubts may emerge about a spouse's commitment, abilities, or intentions. Past wounds, unmet promises, or a lack of emotional or spiritual connection can fuel these doubts, causing tension in the relationship.

Self-Doubt

A partner may also experience self-doubt, questioning their ability to fulfill their role as a spouse, provider, or spiritual leader. This uncertainty often stems from feelings of inadequacy or guilt about perceived failures, which can damage self-confidence and, in turn, the marriage.

Doubt in God's Plan

At times, life's unexpected hardships—infertility, financial struggles, illness, or the loss of a loved one—may test a couple's faith. During these moments, it's normal to question why God allows such challenges or to wonder about His intentions. This spiritual crisis can spill over into the marriage, especially if prayers feel unanswered or life seems unjust.

But doubt need not be seen as a purely negative force. When handled constructively, doubt can become a catalyst for growth and transformation.

Turning Doubt into Growth

Facing doubt honestly can lead to open communication, inviting couples to discuss insecurities and work together to address them. This vulnerability can deepen intimacy and trust, turning doubt into an opportunity for growth and clarity. By sharing concerns and fears, couples can bridge the gap between doubt and faith, strengthening their commitment to each other and to God's plan for their marriage.

Constructive engagement with doubt is ultimately a powerful step toward unwavering faith, which serves as the cornerstone for restoration and resilience in the marital journey. Through faith, couples can renew their bond, emerging stronger and more unified against the challenges of life.

Importance of Unwavering Faith in the Restoration Process

Marriage embodies togetherness, love, and mutual respect, serving as a sacred covenant that binds two individuals in a lifelong commitment. Regardless of whether it arises from secular or Christian traditions, marriage is an invaluable bond. Yet, like any relationship, it can face challenges that may lead to emotional estrangement or even separation. In such instances, the restoration process requires endurance, understanding, and a powerful force—unwavering faith.

To restore trust, heal wounds, and reaffirm commitment, unwavering faith is essential, whether you approach the restoration process from a Christian or secular viewpoint. This chapter delves into the significance of faith in the healing process of marriages for both Christian and non-Christian couples.

Unwavering Faith in Christian Homes

The Covenant of Sacredness

In Christianity, marriage is regarded as a divine covenant. This idea is profoundly illustrated in Genesis 2:24 (NIV):

"That is why a man leaves his father and mother and is united to his wife, and they become one flesh."

Marriage transcends a mere social contract; it is a divinely ordained spiritual connection. When challenges arise in this sacred union, Christians are encouraged to lean on their faith for restoration. Unwavering faith in God is vital during difficult times, as He is seen as the architect of marriage.

The Role of Unwavering Faith in Restoration

Prayer as a Source of Strength: When a marriage struggles, faith manifests through prayer for divine guidance. The Bible encourages Christian couples to pray earnestly, trusting that God will respond in His perfect timing. Philippians 4:6-7 (NIV) states:

"Do not be anxious about anything, but in every situation, by prayer and petition, with thanksgiving, present your requests to God. And the peace of God, which transcends all understanding, will guard your hearts and your minds in Christ Jesus."

Here, prayer serves as a way to invite God into the restoration process, placing trust in Him to heal wounds that may seem irreparable.

Trusting in God's Healing Power: Restoring a marriage often means addressing deep emotional wounds. Even in seemingly hopeless situations, faith empowers believers to trust in God's capacity to heal. Jeremiah 30:17 (NIV) reassures us:

"But I will restore you to health and heal your wounds, declares the Lord."

This promise encompasses both emotional and spiritual healing, reinforcing the belief that God can redeem any marriage, no matter how broken.

Forgiveness through Faith: Unwavering faith is crucial for fostering forgiveness, a fundamental aspect of marital restoration. Ephesians 4:32 (NIV) reminds Christians to:

"Be kind and compassionate to one another, forgiving each other, just as in Christ God forgave you."

Without faith, forgiveness can be a challenge, as the human heart tends to cling to resentment. However, through faith, couples can extend the same grace that God offers them, laying a new foundation for their marriage based on reconciliation and rebirth.

Faith to Persevere: Restoring a marriage is rarely a straightforward or quick process. Faith provides the strength necessary to navigate challenging circumstances. James 1:12 (NIV) emphasizes perseverance:

"Blessed is the one who perseveres under trial because, having stood the test, that person will receive the crown of life that the Lord has promised to those who love him."

This scripture encourages Christians to keep fighting for their marriages, reassuring them that God rewards perseverance.

God's Plan for Reconciliation

Christians are called to view marriage as a bond that deserves protection and nurturing. Malachi 2:16 (NIV) states that God despises divorce:

"'I hate divorce,' says the Lord God of Israel."

This declaration underscores the importance of marriage and the necessity of striving for reconciliation. The aim should always be restoration, grounded in unwavering faith in God's ability to repair what has been broken.

Unwavering Faith in Non-Christian Marriages

Unwavering faith plays a crucial role in the restoration process, even in marriages where the couple did not initially seek God's intervention or identify as Christians. Secular couples often rely on their commitment to the union and the intrinsic value of their relationship, even if they do not perceive their marriage as a divine covenant.

Faith in the Strength of Devotion and Love

Couples who do not seek God may place their faith in the enduring power of love and devotion. While lacking a formal godly framework, principles such as forgiveness, commitment, and understanding are universal. Restoring a strained marriage often begins with a belief in the strength of human love. The secular perspective hinges on the idea that the love that initially united the couple can triumph over their present challenges.

Faith in the Healing or Restoration Process

Unwavering confidence in the healing journey is vital for non-Christian spouses. They may not believe in divine intervention but often trust in therapeutic methods such as communication, self-improvement, and counseling. Many secular couples commit to personal growth and understanding, hoping for a revival in their marriage.

Healing emotional wounds necessitates faith in counseling and therapy or even simple introspection. Secular couples often prioritize open communication and the willingness to evolve, believing that their relationship can be restored through these efforts.

Trust in Collaboration

Trusting that both partners will actively engage in the restoration process is another essential element. A marriage cannot heal unless both spouses are willing to invest in its recovery. Although secular couples may not pray for divine intervention, they often believe in each other's ability to grow, change, and recommit to the relationship. This shared vision for the future and mutual trust are critical to the restoration process. Rebuilding trust is essential; it involves believing that both partners can change, forgive, and move forward.

Key Elements of Marital Restoration

Regardless of the perspective—secular or Christian—several concepts are vital to marital restoration:

- **Patience:** Restoration demands patience, whether relying on God's timing or the healing process.
- **Forgiveness:** The capacity to forgive is essential for both Christian and non-Christian couples. Whether motivated by love or spiritual conviction, forgiveness is crucial for progress.
- **Hope:** Hope—the belief that a relationship can be mended and that brighter days lie ahead—is the bedrock of unwavering faith.

Unwavering faith is crucial to the healing process in both Christian and non-Christian marriages. Christians trust in God's ability to mend, guide, and renew their unions. Through prayer, forgiveness, and perseverance, they believe God is at work in their marriages. Conversely, non-Christian couples rely on faith in love, cooperation, and healing methods. Their dedication to one another and trust in their relationship can help them navigate difficult times, even in the absence of Godly practice.

Regardless of the path taken, a broken marriage can be restored through unwavering faith in the power of healing. This journey can transform suffering into renewed commitment and love. However, when doubt creeps in, it can hinder God's plans for the marriage, delaying the healing that both partners seek.

Doubt Delays the Work of God

In the context of Christian marriage, it is vital to recognize that it is more than just a union of two individuals; it is a covenant partnership anchored in a relationship with God. The principles of togetherness, love, and mutual support form the foundation of God's intention for marriage. However, amidst the trials and tribulations that often test this unity, doubt can subtly infiltrate relationships. This doubt may manifest as uncertainty regarding God's power to save the marriage, as well as skepticism about oneself or one's spouse. Such doubt can significantly delay the work that God desires to accomplish within the marriage.

While doubt is a natural human emotion, it can hinder the ability to fully embrace God's promises and witness His transformative power in marital restoration. Through biblical insights that highlight the detrimental effects of doubt and the empowering nature of faith, we understand that doubt not only delays God's work in marriage but can actively oppose it.

Doubt erodes faith and diminishes confidence in God's capabilities, effectively becoming a barrier to the full manifestation of His actions in a marriage. It undermines trust, disrupts unity, and stifles spiritual growth, all of which can greatly slow or even halt God's work in a marital relationship. God's purpose in marriage is to foster a bond based on love, trust, and mutual dependence, thereby providing a solid foundation for spiritual growth. However, doubt introduces confusion, obstructing this divine purpose and often leading to emotional and spiritual repercussions for both partners involved.

The Quiet Onset of Doubt

Doubt frequently begins in a subtle manner, starting with a small sense of unease regarding oneself, one's spouse, or even God's intentions for the marriage. If this skepticism is left unaddressed, it can intensify, impacting attitudes and behaviors that ultimately affect the relationship. A breakdown in trust may arise as partners begin to question each other's commitment, capabilities, or intentions. This erosion of trust is particularly damaging, as trust is crucial for opening hearts to spiritual guidance. The absence of trust not only disrupts emotional bonds but also complicates God's ability to work within the marriage.

When doubt takes hold, it can make believing in God's purpose more challenging. In the absence of faith, partners may rely more on their own judgment than on divine insight, leading to decisions that diverge from God's intentions for their relationship. For instance, when faced with difficulties, couples might succumb to despair instead of viewing challenges as opportunities for growth or turning to prayer and support from each other. Such doubt can prevent one or both partners from progressing in their faith, thereby obstructing the spiritual and relational development that God desires for them.

Communication Breakdown

Doubt also creates barriers to communication, which is crucial for a healthy marriage. If one partner harbors doubt about the other's commitment or intentions, they may hesitate to communicate openly, leading to misunderstandings and emotional disconnection. This lack of transparency can leave each partner feeling isolated, misunderstood, and undervalued, which may spiral into a cycle of escalating doubt. As communication deteriorates, the couple's ability to resolve conflicts and grow spiritually together diminishes.

Nevertheless, Scripture encourages Christians to place their full trust in God rather than relying on their own understanding, as seen in Proverbs 3:5–6. When doubt infiltrates a marriage, it indicates a lack of faith in God's abilities and purposes. God invites couples to surrender their doubts, recognizing that His ways are higher and His plans for them are good, as stated in Jeremiah 29:11. By releasing uncertainty and embracing trust, couples can allow God to work within their marriage, facilitating healing, harmony, and growth.

Doubt obstructs God's work in marriage by creating barriers between partners and between the couple and God. However, couples can overcome their doubts and fulfill God's design for their relationship by choosing to trust, communicate openly, and seek divine guidance in all circumstances. When faith supplants doubt, couples can cultivate a thriving, purpose-filled marriage that honors God, enabling Him to work effectively within their lives. This transformation allows partners to experience the fulfillment and joy that come from a strong marital bond anchored in unwavering faith.

How to Handle the Enemy's Attacks on Your Faith

Understanding that doubt can hinder God's work in our lives and marriages are crucial for couples seeking spiritual resilience. To effectively counter the enemy's attacks, it is essential to cultivate spiritual awareness, establish a solid foundation in God's Word, and engage in persistent faith-building practices. Since faith is the cornerstone of a Christian's relationship with God, it often becomes the primary target of the adversary's assaults. Fortunately, Scripture provides us with powerful tools and guidance to withstand these attacks, maintain our faith, and remain steadfast.

1. Recognize the Nature of the Enemy's Attack

The primary objective of the enemy is succinctly stated in Scripture: to steal, kill, and destroy (John 10:10). The adversary frequently launches assaults through doubt, anxiety, confusion, discouragement, and temptation. These tactics aim to weaken a believer's connection with God, erode their faith in His promises, and create a sense of isolation during hardships. To mount an effective resistance, it is crucial to understand the intentional and calculated nature of these attacks.

2. Put on the Whole Armor of God

In Ephesians 6:10–18, Apostle Paul instructs Christians to put on the "whole armor of God" to withstand the schemes of the devil. This armor comprises:

- **The Belt of Truth**: This component helps us remain grounded in God's truth, enabling us to discern the lies of the adversary.
- **The Breastplate of Righteousness**: By living morally, we shield our hearts from shame and guilt, which the enemy uses to chip away at our faith.
- **The Shoes of the Gospel of Peace**: This equips us to resist the tension and fear that the adversary employs to manipulate us.
- **The Shield of Faith**: This protective barrier guards us against the enemy's flaming darts of discouragement, fear, and doubt.
- **The Helmet of Salvation**: Our identity in Christ fortifies our minds against the enemy's deceptions and accusations.
- **The Sword of the Spirit**: Scripture serves as our weapon to dispel falsehoods and reaffirm God's promises.

By actively engaging this spiritual armor, we boost our defenses and safeguard our faith against attacks.

3. Respond to the Attacks of the Enemy Using God's Word

Jesus exemplified the power of God's Word in Matthew 4:1–11, where He resisted each of Satan's temptations while in the wilderness. This episode illustrates that

Scripture is a formidable defense against demonic assaults. By memorizing verses that reflect God's character and affirm His promises, believers equip themselves to combat the enemy's attempts to undermine their faith.

4. Stand Firm in Prayer

Prayer serves as a crucial line of defense against the adversary of your faith. In Philippians 4:6-7, Paul encourages Christians to present their requests to God through prayer and thanksgiving, assuring that "the peace of God, which transcends all understanding, will guard your hearts and minds in Christ Jesus." Regular prayer invites God's presence and protection into our struggles, strengthening our faith and diminishing the enemy's influence. Additionally, Paul underscores the significance of prayer as vital armor in our spiritual battles in Ephesians 6:18, where he advocates praying in the Spirit at all times for all types of requests. Persistent prayer nurtures our faith and deepens our relationship with God, making it increasingly difficult for the adversary to shake our foundation.

5. Guard Your Heart

The adversary frequently targets believers through their thoughts, sowing confusion and despair. Proverbs 4:23 reminds us to "guard our hearts, for everything we do flows from it." By being mindful of what we expose ourselves to—such as toxic relationships, negative media, and damaging conversations—we can protect our hearts. Philippians 4:8 encourages believers to focus on what is true, noble, right, pure, lovely, and admirable. By concentrating on these positive attributes, we safeguard ourselves from the enemy's efforts to instill negativity and hopelessness.

6. Embrace a Community Driven by Faith

Isolation can make us more vulnerable to the enemy's attacks on our faith. In Hebrews 10:24-25, Christians are urged to support one another and "not give up meeting together." Surrounding ourselves with fellow believers allows us to encourage, uplift, and hold each other accountable. When our faith is tested, a community of Christians helps reinforce our resolve and serves as a reminder of God's faithfulness. By sharing our victories and struggles, we fortify our defenses against spiritual assaults and enhance our collective faith.

7. Walk by Faith, Not by Sight

The enemy often exploits circumstances to undermine our faith, creating the illusion that God is indifferent or distant from our needs. In contrast, Paul urges us in 2 Corinthians 5:7 to "walk by faith, not by sight." This means we should trust in God's promises, even when immediate answers or comfort are lacking. We must cling to the assurance that

God is trustworthy and orchestrates everything for our ultimate good (Romans 8:28). By focusing on God's promises rather than our present challenges, we resist the enemy's attempts to shake our faith.

8. Affirm Your Victory through Jesus Christ

It is vital to remember that Christ has already secured victory over the enemy that attacks our faith. The enemy desires for us to confess defeat, but God calls us to declare our victory in faith. As stated in Colossians 2:15, Jesus disarmed the rulers and authorities through His death on the cross. This victory signifies that we fight from a position of triumph, not loss. In the face of challenges to our faith, we can confidently declare that "greater is He who is in you than he who is in the world" (1 John 4:4). Remembering that Jesus has already won the ultimate battle empowers us to remain steadfast and strengthens our commitment to resist the adversary's attacks on our faith.

By implementing these strategies, couples can take an active role in defending their faith against the enemy's assaults. Through awareness, prayer, community support, and a strong grounding in Scripture, we can navigate the trials that threaten our spiritual connection and marital harmony, emerging victorious in the grace and strength of God.

Prayer point

Heavenly Father, we approach your throne in all humility, we acknowledge that our restoration process in our marriage depends on our unwavering faith. Please, help us to let go of doubt that impedes Your work in our lives and marriage, increase our faith and teach us to rely on Your promises thereby resisting the enemy's attacks on our faith. Help us to stay rooted in Your Word so that our faith in You remains unwavering and we may receive what You have planned for us in Jesus' name, Amen.

Chapter 3

Self-Evaluation – The First Step To Healing

ow, let me reiterate that marriage breakdowns can be very painful, but the good news is; healing is possible. The subject of faith earlier discussed told us that. Faith will not only defend your marriage, but also help you go on the offensive against satanic onslaught. I guess you learned so much from the previous chapter.

Now that you have faith, and believe that there's something God can do about your broken marriage, the first and most important step to healing is self-evaluation that is taking a deep, introspective look at your role in the relationship and how your actions or inactions may have contributed to its decline. This chapter focuses on how to engage in meaningful self-reflection, uncover your shortcomings, and seek grace from God for all round transformation for not just your marriage but also your life.

Throughout this chapter, you will be exposed to prompts that will help you uncover your faults in the breakdown of your marriage. I won't promise you that it will be easy, however it will be a starting point for the restoration of your marriage.

Addressing Your Own Role in the Breakdown of the Marriage

Marriage involves two individuals coming together, each with their own temperaments, background, strengths, weaknesses and expectations (realistic and nonrealistic). Problems arise when the two people involved do not know how to manage each other's personality and to meet their needs. When these problems arise, it's tempting to blame your spouse entirely, but true healing can only begin when you first take a look at your own behaviors that may have contributed to the breakdown of your marriage. This will be a good time to reflect on your behaviors and reactions during conflicts. Ask yourself questions like:

- How did I respond to my spouse's needs?

- Was I dismissive or overly critical?

- Did I prioritize my own feelings over my spouse's?

This process requires a lot of patience, emotional maturity and honesty. Let's look at a couple of other things you need to keep in mind.

1. Recognizing Patterns of Blame

Blame is one of the biggest obstacles to self-evaluation. When we focus on what our spouse did wrong, it becomes harder to see our own part in the problem. Blame shifts responsibility, but true growth comes from taking ownership of our actions. Remember how Adam was quick to blame Eve when God asked him why he ate the forbidden fruit? That's exactly what I mean. He didn't remember that he was the one instructed not to eat of the fruit in the garden. He was quick to point a finger at Eve. That's how blame shifting blinds our ability to see our own faults when resolving issues. Acknowledging your role doesn't mean taking all the blame. Instead, it's about recognizing how your actions, words, or lack of communication may have impacted the relationship.

Reflection Prompt 1: When things went wrong, how often did I blame my spouse instead of looking at my own actions? Was I quick to point fingers, or did I take a step back to see if I contributed to the issue?

2. How Did You Handle Disagreements?

Think about your past arguments or disagreements. How did you respond to the conflicts? Did you remain calm and seek resolution, or did you retreat during arguments or become defensive or aggressive and tend to escalate them? Sometimes, we carry unresolved personal issues into our marriage, making us more reactive than we should be.

Personal Example: Recall a disagreement that escalated quickly. What was the trigger? Reflect on your behavior—did you raise your voice, shut down, or retaliate? Could the outcome have been different if you had approached it differently? Most times, our responses to conflict often mirror our internal struggles. By understanding our triggers and reactions, we can start to unlearn negative patterns and develop healthier ways of handling disagreements.

3. Unmet Expectations and Communication Breakdowns

Many marital issues stem from unmet expectations—either spoken or unspoken. Perhaps you expected your spouse to support you in a certain way, but they didn't. Or they promised to change in certain areas and they didn't sooner like you expected then you became reactive or withdrawn. Or maybe you wanted them to "just know" how you were feeling, without clearly communicating your needs. Now, consider the expectations you have for yourself and your partner. Are they realistic? Sometimes, we project our desires onto our spouse without considering their needs or limitations.

Reflection Prompt 2: In what ways did I fail to communicate my needs? Did I assume my spouse should just understand what I wanted without having to ask? Was I patient enough in allowing my spouse to adjust to meeting my needs?

Personal Example: Reflect on a time when you felt disappointed or let down in your marriage. Did you openly express your feelings, or did you harbor resentment? Could clearer communication have prevented misunderstandings? Think about it!

4. External Stressors and Their Impact

External stressors like work pressure, financial strain, or even extended family can create significant challenges in marriages. Think about your own experiences: How often do you bring work frustrations home? When you're stressed, do you notice yourself becoming irritable or withdrawn? Also, consider the impact of financial challenges. Are you and your spouse communicating openly about money? If you find yourselves arguing about finances, ask yourself: How can I contribute to a more constructive conversation?

Health issues can also shift the balance in a relationship. Do you feel overwhelmed by caregiving responsibilities? How might you better support your partner during difficult times?

And what about family dynamics? Are you prioritizing your spouse's needs, or do family expectations sometimes create division? Reflect on these questions to understand how external stressors may have influenced your relationship. Taking responsibility can pave the way for healing and help you rebuild a stronger connection.

Reflection Prompt 3: Were there times when I allowed external pressures to take priority over my relationship? How did I cope with stress, and did I inadvertently take it out on my spouse? Did I make any decision or take any action from external influence like family and friends whether knowingly or unknowingly?

Write Out the Areas You Did Wrong

Self-evaluation is most powerful when it's done in writing. The act of putting thoughts to paper forces us to be honest with ourselves in ways that mere thinking doesn't. Even the Word of God supports that we write down visions so that we can run with it. Habakkuk 2;2

1. The Importance of Writing for Clarity

When you write down the areas where you may have gone wrong, you gain clarity. You see the patterns in your behavior and identify the specific actions or attitudes that contributed to the breakdown of the relationship. This exercise helps you confront uncomfortable truths, but it's also the first step toward change.

For Example: Take a specific incident where you know you could have acted differently. Describe it in detail, including how you felt at the time, how you reacted, and what the outcome was. Then, reflect on how you might approach a similar situation in the future.

2. Prompts for Self-Reflection

To help guide your writing, here are several prompts to dive deeper into your behavior and mindset:

a. How did I show love to my spouse on a daily basis? Did I make an effort to express my love, or did I assume my spouse knew how I felt?

b. Was I emotionally available? Did I create a space where my spouse felt safe to share their thoughts and feelings, or was I distant or dismissive?

c. How did I handle my own emotional needs? Did I communicate when I felt neglected or hurt, or did I suppress my emotions, leading to resentment?

d. Did I contribute to emotional disconnection? Over time, emotional disconnection can lead to the breakdown of a relationship. Think about whether you contributed to this by withdrawing, being overly critical, or failing to nurture the relationship.

3. Owning Your Imperfections

The goal here isn't to beat yourself up but to acknowledge your imperfections. Writing out where you went wrong helps you take responsibility and gives you a clearer path toward healing.

Example: Recall a recurring argument in your marriage. What was your role in that argument? Did you approach it with a closed mind or a willingness to resolve it?

Prayer against Negative Attitudes

Healing is not just about self-awareness. It's also about seeking grace for transformation. Prayer is a powerful tool that allows us to surrender our shortcomings and ask for God's assistance in changing our attitudes and behaviors. Hebrews 4:16, Romans 12:2

1. Why We Need Grace

Grace gives us the strength to confront our flaws without becoming overwhelmed by guilt. It reminds us that change is possible and that we are not alone in our journey toward healing. When we pray for grace, we are asking for the humility to recognize our faults and the courage to make amends. Self-evaluation can be painful, but through grace, you can turn that pain into growth. Grace allows you to see your mistakes, but it also provides the hope and strength to become a better person.

2. Prayers for Transformation

"Lord, I come to You, humbled by the realization of my flaws and shortcomings. I recognize that I have contributed to the breakdown of my marriage in ways that I may not have fully understood until now. I ask for Your grace to guide me as I confront these parts of myself that need healing. Help me to release the pride, anger, and bitterness that have clouded my heart and mind. Show me how to love with patience, communicate with kindness, and act with humility. Where there was once defensiveness, let there be openness. Where there was once harshness, let there be gentleness. I ask for the strength to change, to grow, and to rebuild. In Your mercy, Lord, grant me the wisdom to learn from my mistakes and the courage to make things right. Amen."

Prayer is not just a passive activity—it's a declaration of your willingness to change. Each time you pray for grace, you are inviting God to walk with you on this journey of self-discovery and healing.

3. Incorporating Prayer into Your Daily Life

Transformation takes time, and that's why it's important to make prayer a regular part of your healing process. Each day, ask for grace not only to change your attitudes but to heal from the pain of the past.

Reflection Prompt 4: As you pray each day, reflect on the changes you are experiencing. Are you becoming more patient, more self-aware, more loving? Write down any positive shifts you notice in your behavior or mindset.

In conclusion, self-evaluation is a necessary step in healing from a marriage breakdown. By honestly addressing your own role, writing down your areas for improvement, and praying for grace to amend negative attitudes, you are taking the first step toward personal growth. Remember, this journey is about progress, not perfection. Healing doesn't happen overnight, but with each step, you are getting closer to becoming the best version of yourself— one that is capable of love, growth, and transformation.

This process may feel overwhelming at times, but it is one of the most empowering journeys you can take. It allows you to reclaim control over your actions, thoughts, and emotions, laying a strong foundation for rebuilding your marriage.

Chapter 4

The Power Of Prayer And Fasting In Restoring Your Marriage

Have you ever felt as if you and your spouse were caught in a never-ending cycle of discord? Although your love for your spouse is genuine, yet there are moments when it seems that no matter what you do or say, things will only get worse. What if I tell you that there is a way to get beyond that obstacle and restore the lovely marriage you once had?

Yes, there is, and it's not as difficult as you imagine. In our journey through the challenges of marriage, one indisputable fact emerges from our experience: the therapeutic and restorative power of prayer and fasting. Even though divorce might be one of life's most agonizing traumas, I've got good news for you, there is hope for recovery.

In the previous chapter, we talked about faith and how it enables you to take on spiritual resistance head-on while also protecting your marriage. We also discussed how self-evaluation, which is the first step towards restoring your marriage, will help to restore the sweetness in the wine of the most difficult marriages that had been long stolen by the devil.

However, in this chapter I'll be unraveling how prayer and fasting serve as an effective means of fostering spiritual transformation in your marriage while also fortifying your bond in marriage when engaged with the right attitude. This approach has been tested, trusted and proven beyond reasonable doubt to put an end to the struggles encountered in marriage is what I am about to share with you in this chapter.

Fasting and prayer from time past acts as a balm for the wounds in marriage, giving room for resentments to subside and deep wounds to heal. They are essential rituals that restore the strong, loving bond between couples as well as their relationship with God. When combined, prayer and fasting springs up a flow of grace and patience that gives couples a new perspective about one another. By engaging in prayer and fasting, miscommunications are cleared up, new wine is restored and joy rediscovered in your marriage.

However, couples should think of fasting as an act of devotion rather than deprivation. It is an act of surrendering your own wants to achieve purpose, direction and clarity in your marriage. Fasting paired with prayer, becomes a strong, deliberate act that gives room for love to flourish because it removes interior clutter in marriage.

In a world full of distractions and ups and downs, this approach is a haven of peace that enables couples to better understand one another's emotions triumphing over the work of the evil one constantly waging war against their union.

Now that we are in the know that prayer and fasting are effective and active tools that we can engage to restore our marriage, there is a need for us to know what prayer and fasting entails so that when engaged it will yield the expected results.

Defining Prayer

Prayer is fundamentally an intimate communion and connection with God. It is a medium to communicate with the Divine, express your innermost feelings, anxieties, hopes, ask for wisdom, courage and healing. Jesus discussed the concept of prayer in Matthew 6:6 in a straightforward and intimate manner:

"But when you pray, go into your room, close the door, and pray to your Father, who is unseen. Then your Father, who sees what is done in secret, will reward you."

Your prayer room can be your prayer altar. Every couple should create or have a space they use for prayer. We often call it, "Family Altar".

Prayer allows couples to bring God into their marriage hence, it is a potent channel of communication.

Additionally, prayer is an expression of our humility. It shows that we acknowledge that God's wisdom surpasses our own and that there are situations that are beyond our control. The scripture in Philippians 4:6-7 explain gave a vivid explanation,

"Do not be anxious about anything, but in every situation, by prayer and supplication, with thanksgiving, present your requests to God. And the peace of God, which transcends all understanding, will guard your hearts and your minds in Christ Jesus."

The soothing and comforting power of prayer is emphasized in this verse; it builds our hearts and offers peace that transcends human understanding, which is crucial for any struggling marriage.

Defining Fasting

The intentional withholding of food, activities, or pleasures for a predetermined period of time in order to focus on prayer, spiritual growth, and building a connection with God is known as fasting. In the scriptures, prayer and fasting are often combined to seek God for wisdom, deliverance, and intervention. The scriptures in Matthew 6:16–18 says,

"When you fast, do not look somber as the hypocrites do, for they disfigure their faces to show others they are fasting… so that it will not be obvious to others that you are fasting, but only to your Father, who is unseen; and your Father, who sees what is done in secret, will reward you."

Fasting is more than just denying oneself of food; it is an act of our devotion to God. Fasting makes room in the physical world for the spiritual to thrive. It helps people become more conscious of God's direction and align their hearts with His will. It is a moment where both spouses humble themselves, reflect on their marriage, seek guidance and healing from God.

Now that you know what fasting and prayers entails, you should know how to engage it and learn how to pray for your spouse and your marriage to ensure that your marriage is able to withstand the storms of life when it rages.

Types of Fasting

Fasting can be classified into different categories base on form or duration. Here're a few types of fasting;

Partial Fast: When engaging in this type of fasting, you're restricted from specific foods or food groups rather than abstaining from all food. Examples include the "Daniel Fast," where people consume only fruits, vegetables, and water, or fasting from certain indulgences (like sweets or caffeine) while still eating a basic diet.

Normal Fast: This type of fasting is often practiced by those who engage in long duration fast. In a normal fast, a person abstains from all food but continues drinking water. This is often done for a specific period, such as a day or a few days, and is commonly practiced in religious or spiritual contexts.

Intermittent Fasting: This is a pattern of fasting; eating is alternated between periods of fasting and eating. For example, in the 16/8 method, a person fasts for 16 hours each day and eats only during an 8-hour window. Other forms include the 5:2 diet, where participants eat normally for five days and restrict calorie intake on two non-consecutive days.

Absolute Fast: In an absolute fast, a person abstains from all food and drink, including water, for a short period. Due to its intensity, this fast is generally done only for a short duration (typically no longer than 1-3 days) and often under specific spiritual conviction or guidance, as it can be physically challenging. Absolute fasts are sometimes done in times of extreme need or urgency, as seen in the Bible with Esther and the people of Nineveh.

Corporate Fast: A corporate fast involves a group of people fasting together for a shared purpose, such as a church congregation or community seeking divine guidance, breakthrough, or spiritual unity. During a corporate fast, participants may choose the same type of fasting, such as a partial or normal fast, or different fasts depending on individual capacity and commitment. This type of fast is often a time of communal prayer, worship, and reflection, enhancing the collective spiritual focus and support.

Learning to Pray for your Marriage

One thing I have learnt over the years is that prayer is not the last resort but the first line of defense against the attack of the devil in restoring marriages. No wonder the enemy is always on the run seeking to find any crack in your marriage so that he will weasel his way into your marriage in the absence of fasting and prayers. However, our formidable weapon of warfare to overcome the whims and tricks of the devil is **Prayer**.

You will agree with me that by learning how to pray for your partner and your marriage, many couples find a deep source of healing and strength during these trying times. It creates a spiritual firm foundation that can withstand any adversity by inviting God's knowledge, peace and presence into your marriage through the weapon of prayer.

The scriptures have provided us with rich instances of how prayer has preserved marriages, resulting in divine intervention and changed lives which I'll share with you as we proceed in this chapter. Praying for your spouse and marriage involves more than just requesting for changes; it also involves encouraging one another, expressing gratitude and asking God for direction. This reminds couples of God's divine design for love and companionship while adding intimacy, and purpose to your marriage.

I'll be discussing how you pray for your spouses and give examples in the scriptures that are written for us to follow. This will ignite you to stand up and fight for your marriage.

Offer prayers for your spouse from a place of love and surrender

To learn how to begin praying for your spouse, you must first of all be willing to surrender them into God's care. This involves putting aside any efforts to correct them and having faith that God is more aware of their needs better than we do. The scriptures encourage us to: *"cast all your anxiety on him because he cares for you."* God operates in our spouse's life in His own perfect time when we approach Him, surrendering our heart, letting go of our worries and concerns.

The Abraham and Sarah Story

You will agree with me that the biblical account of Abraham and Sarah serves as a powerful illustration of prayer and submission. Despite a protracted time of uncertainty and waiting, Abraham remained confident in God's promises for his family. God promised Abraham that he would become the father of many nations in Genesis 15 and he remained steadfast. Abraham's dedication to prayer and faith in God's plan for his spouse serves as a reminder of how, even in the face of seemingly insurmountable obstacles, submitting our marriage to God results in divine fulfillment.

Learning to pray for your spouse, allow God to guide and shape them according to His will. This is an act of total submission. Allow God's love to work in your lives together by letting go of all expectations and control.

Ask for protection and strength

One of the best ways to support your spouse is to pray for strength and protection for them. Life often presents us with a number of challenges, including responsibilities to one's marriage, health conditions, unemployment and so on. When we pray for strength for our spouse's, we're telling God to give them courage and wisdom at their most vulnerable moments.

Psalm 91:11–12 is a beautiful prayer for protection:

"For he will command his angels concerning you to guard you in all your ways; they will lift you up in their hands, so that you will not strike your foot against a stone."

While praying, ask God to surround your spouse with His angels and give them the peace and confidence they need to face any challenges in marriage.

The Ruth and Boaz Story

One of the best examples of God's provision and protectionin marriage is seen in the story of Ruth and Boaz. Despitetheir struggles, Ruth, a Moabite widow, decided to remain with her mother-in-law, Naomi. Ruth's loyalty brought her into contact with Boaz, a gentle and honorable guy who looked out for her. Their story demonstrates how, even amid trying circumstances, God still provides love, safety, and strength in marriage till today.

When you pray for your spouse's safety and strength, keep in mind Boaz's devotion and Ruth's resilience. Ask God to keep your spouse strong in faith, guard their heart, mind, and spirit.

Ask for discernment and wisdom

In marriage, you will agree with me that we all have times when we require discernment to make the right choices. Your spouse gets direction and clarity for the decisions they must make when you pray for wisdom for them. James 1:5 serves as a reminder for us in case we have forgotten that,

"If any of you lacks wisdom, you should ask God, who gives generously to all without finding fault, and it will be given to you."

When you pray to God to give your spouse wisdom, you make room for divine understanding and strengthen your marriage.

The Story of Esther

Esther's story serves as a powerful illustration of how prayer and seeking wisdom can alter the path of history. Esther fasted and prayed to God for direction after hearing about Haman's plan to exterminate her people. In addition to saving her people, Esther's readiness to seek God's counsel increased her bravery and strength. Her experience brings to our consciousness that asking God for wisdom results in God's intervention in any situation in our marriage.

When you pray for wisdom for your spouse, you're asking God to give them insight, clarity and understanding. Ask God to lead them in their career, relationships, spiritual development and to keep them open to hearing from Him.

Pray for Unity and Forgiveness

The foundation of every long-lasting marriage is forgiveness. Restoring love and peace in your marriage requires both of you to pray for your own capacity to forgive and for your spouse's heart to become softened and more receptive to forgive. The scriptures in Ephesians 4:32 encourage us to:

"Be kind and compassionate to one another, forgiving each other, just as in Christ God forgave you."

When you pray for your spouse, you're telling God to take away your pride, wrath, bitterness and replace them with the spirit of peace and love in your marriage.

The Prodigal Son's Parable

The prodigal son parable in (Luke 15:11–32) is a lovely example of reconciliation and forgiveness. In this parable, the father welcomes his son back with open arms and absolves him of every shortcoming without harboring any form of resentment. In the same vein, God commands us to love and care for our spouses and to forgive them when they offend us. We learn from the Father's example that genuine forgiveness is a decision to love despite one's flaws and shortcomings; it is unconditional.

Ask God to instill the spirit of forgiveness in your spouse while you pray. Ask Him to help you and your spouse let go of the past so that grace and love will grow in your marriage.

Pray for Spiritual Growth

Praying for your spouse's spiritual growth is one of the most heartfelt ways to help them. As you both get more intimate with God, you will discover that your bond becomes stronger. A power-packed prayer for spiritual growth is found in Colossians 1:9–10.

"We continually ask God to fill you with the knowledge of his will through all the wisdom and understanding that the Spirit gives, so that you may live a life worthy of the Lord and please him in every way."

The purpose of this prayer is to ask God to deepen your spouse's faith and lead them to a deeper relationship with Him.

Aquila and Priscilla's Story

As a married couple in the New Testament, Priscilla and Aquila devoted their lives to sharing the gospel. In close collaboration with Apostle Paul, they used their house as a center of worship and teaching. They serve as a wonderful example of a couple spiritually united in marriage because of their love, dedication and faith in God. Their story is an example of a marriage where couples grow from faith to faith. For your spouse's spiritual growth, pray that God strengthens their bond with Him. Learn to pray that your spouse pursues God's will in everything, that their faith inspires and brings them joy.

Pray for affection and love

You will agree with me that it's critical to preserve love, and companionship in marriage. Praying for your spouse's love is a reminder to both of you to place value in expressing love on a regular basis. The virtues of love are beautifully explained in 1 Corinthians 13:4–7:

"Love is patient, love is kind. It does not envy, it does not boast, it is not proud. It does not dishonor others; it is not self-seeking..."

This scripture reminds couples to pray that the love of God will continue to be the driving force in their marriage.

Jacob and Rachel's Story

The strength of love and dedication is seen in the account of Jacob and Rachel (Genesis 29). Jacob willingly worked for fourteen years because he was so devoted to and loved Rachel. His perseverance and commitment demonstrate how love can motivate and persist even in the face of prolonged waiting. Jacob's love serves as a reminder that genuine affection entails loving and cherishing one another in spite of challenges.

In order to reaffirm your love and commitment to one another, ask God to assist you and your spouse to treat each other with compassion. Ask God to keep you focused on the happiness and beauty of your marriage.

Learning to pray for your partner and marriage is one ofthe most fulfilling and life-changing things couples engagein. Prayer fortifies your union and brings peace, love and understanding into your marriage when you invite God into your marriage. Always remember that God is attentive to genuine prayers, regardless of whether you're asking for knowledge, forgiveness, or spiritual growth in your home. With perseverance, commitment, faith and trust you will see God's hand at work, strengthening your union and bringing you both nearer to Him.

Would you be serious with praying for your spouse today? Are you willing to go all-out for your marriage? Are you willing to cry unto God until your marriage becomes heaven on earth? How badly do you want to do this?

The Role of Fasting in Fighting for Your Marriage

Sometimes, in spite of our best efforts, we encounter difficulties in marriage that seem insurmountable. In some case, some marriages even get to a point of separation; where either the man or the wife walks away. The truth is, Even the strongest of relationships suffers from disagreements, miscommunications and adversity. Fasting is a powerful tool for Christians, a biblically based practice that invokes God's power, wisdom, and involvement in our marriage. It is a powerful tool of devotion and commitment that invokes God to intervene profoundly in our marriage and lives, resolving problems that would seem insurmountable on our own.

Fasting has a special function in Christian marriage because it creates a spiritual space where God operates unhindered when combined with prayer. This practice is a life-changing procedure that cleanses our hearts, renews our perspective and brings us closer to God, our spouse, and His designs for our marriage. It is more than just a means of **"fixing"** our marriage

Hence, fasting in marriage cannot be overemphasized, especially in this era where divorce has become the new normal. Fasting is a potent spiritual exercise that has been proven to strengthen and revitalize marriages that are at the edge. Knowing what exactly fasting does in your marriage will enable you and your spouse to engage it without fail.

I have seen situations where already separated couples came back together by virtue of a resilient attitude of one of the partners. She fasted and trusted God for absolute restoration of her marriage, and the Lord did it. Faith in God is indeed the key to unlocking insurmountable challenges.

Fasting is a powerful and faith-based strategy for believers to fight for their marriage. In a society where Christian couples constantly face many spiritual and physical obstacles, fasting becomes an effective strategy to ask God for help, strengthen marital ties, and fight spiritual battles against influences that seek to break the union and sanctity of marriage. I'll be unraveling biblical examples on how you can fight for your marriage and also share with you, concrete and biblical ways that fasting assist Christians couples in fighting for their marriage:

Reliance on God and Humility

Fasting is an act of submission, a means to put our marriage in God's hands to show that we depend on Him. The scriptures in 2 Chronicles 20:3-4, talks about King Jehoshaphat declaring a fast when his people were threatened by other nations of the world. The king displayed humility and reliance on God in (2 Chronicles 20:12)*"We do not know what to do, but our eyes are on you"*. Fasting enables couples to humble themselves, which in return gives room for God's grace and favor. It plays the role of overcoming the natural selfishness of human nature that couples often exhibit which often lead to conflict in marriages. In a similar vein, when we fast for our marriage, we acknowledge that we do not have answers to all our questions, but we put our faith in God's integrity to repair and heal our marriage.

It Makes room for Wisdom and Spiritual Clarity

Fasting reduces external distractions, which helps us focus on God's instructions and directions. We observe fast because we have the understanding that it is intended to *"lose the chains of injustice...to set the oppressed free and break every yoke,"* according to the scriptures in (Isaiah 58:6). Fasting reveals marital issues that we may not have previously noticed or didn't see as an issue, it teaches us how to fix them. Through fasting, the Holy Spirit shows us where we need to change, forgive, or have a deeper understanding of our spouse.

Overcoming Challenges and Fostering Spiritual Growth

Disputes in marriage that involve more serious issues can sometimes resemble spiritual battles. Fasting is one proven method for conquering spiritual obstacles. The scriptures in Mark 9:29, *"This kind can come out only by prayer and fasting,"* this speaks of a challenging situation that can only be surmounted when we engage fast.

When combined with prayer, fasting becomes a potent tool for defending your marriage, tearing down barriers of mistrust, anger, and bitterness paving the way for God's transformational power to reign.

It Builds Closer Relationships with God and One's Spouse

Fasting builds one's closeness with God and one's spouse. Couples establish a foundation based on mutual dependence on God, humility and spiritual discipline as they fast and pray together. Being closer to God inevitably leads to a closer bond with one another, which promotes harmony and focus on divine direction. Jesus reminds couples that God's presence is apparent when they seek Him together in Matthew 18:19–20 when He said, *"Where two or three gather in my name, there am I with them.* Fasting breaches the gap between couples and God thereby rendering the plan of the devil in your marriage non-effect.

Healing and Spiritual Purification

Fasting as an act of purification, encourages couples to be knitted to God and seek His healing to cure their marital scars. It is common for unresolved wounds, animosity, or old grudges to cause discord. Fasting enables couples to humble themselves before God, let go of their worries, ask for pardon and emotional healing. The scripture clearly explains this in Isaiah 58:6;

"Is not this the kind of fasting I have chosen: to lose the chains of injustice and untie the cords of the yoke, to set the oppressed free and break every yoke?"

In marriage, fasting plays the role of delivering spouses from the **"yokes"** of bitterness, past hurts they hold in their hearts, or misunderstandings, giving room for God's healing to restore love and peace.

Spiritual Warfare Against the Enemy

Due to the fact that Christian marriages symbolize the love and commitment between Christ and the Church, their marriages are often attacked. Prayers are a potent weapon in spiritual battle and it becomes more intense when it goes hand in hand with fasting. Certain spiritual warfare can only be conquered when we engage **"prayer and fasting,"** which is also written in the scriptures. This directly relates to defending our marriage against spiritual onslaught like temptation, misunderstandings, or conflict. The scripture makes it clear in Ephesians 6:12, *"For we do not wrestle against flesh and blood, but against principalities, against powers, against the rulers of the darkness of this age, against spiritual hosts of wickedness in the heavenly places"*. This is an indicator that fasting is a vital weapon couples who seek to fulfill God's mandate for marriage **MUST** engage.

Fasting helps in knowing God's Will and Guidance

Sometimes lack of direction or alignment with God's plan is the root cause of marital difficulties. Couples should engage fasting to seek the face of God for will before making any choices in all areas of life. By allowing God to take the **LEAD** in our marriage, fasting helps couples realign their marriages according to His purpose, (read Proverbs 3:5-6). This promotes togetherness and gives couples the knowledge they need to overcome challenges in marriage.

Fasting Invites God's Blessings and Favor in Marriage

Fasting as a medium to committing one's marriage to God, praying for His favor, provision, and His blessings. When spouses fast, they open their marriage to God's miraculous benefits, believing Him to supply, heal, and secure their marriage (Isaiah 58:9). God promises to respond to those who fast and pray fervently. Fasting allows couples to put their confidence in God's provision, which strengthens their marriage with His protection and favor.

Fasting helps in cultivating a heart of gratitude and contentment.

Many marriages nowadays are threatened by unhappiness and the act of comparison. Fasting plays the role of helping Christians spouses shift their attention away from worldly distractions, fostering a sense of thankfulness for their spouses and satisfaction in their marriage. This shields your marriage against extraneous sources of unhappiness or discontentment. The scriptures urge us to: *"Give thanks in all circumstances; for this is God's will for you in Christ Jesus"* (1 Thessalonians 5:18). Fasting helps couples give thanks to God for bringing them together which increases contentment and joy in the marriage making it resilient to external pressures.

Practical Tips for Fasting in Marriage you need to apply

- ***Take decisions together:*** Make it a habit to agree as a couple on specified times to fast and pray for your marriage. Ensure that you're both on the same page so that your fast will not be a hunger strike and your prayers hindered.
- ***Be purposeful:*** Have a set time and agree together on the purpose for the fast, maybe it's for healing, unity, protection, guidance, etc., before embarking on it.

- ***Be intentional about your prayers:*** Ask the Holy Spirit to identify and mend specific areas in your marriage. Better still, mention the areas in the place of prayers and pray with the intention of seeing a positive result.

- ***Read the scripture together:*** Meditate on verses that promote faith, love, unity, and confidence in God's promises. Reading the scriptures together enables you to speak life and God's light to your marriage and all that concerns you.

- ***Encourage one another:*** Fasting may be difficult; encourage one another and celebrate tiny wins in faith.

- ***Trust God's time:*** God has His own time. Be patient, knowing that He is working both in your hearts and marriage until it is conformed to His will.

In a world that often undermines godly marriages, fasting provides a way for couples to strengthen their relationship and develop spiritually. Fasting together as couples allows Christian couples to take a stance against spiritual dangers as well as accepting God's power to protect, heal, and transform their marriage according to His plan.

Fasting plays a major role in putting your marriage in God's care during difficult times and relying on Him for healing, insight, and a fresh start. It is a heavenly act of faith that strengthens your marriage to weather any storm culminating in the restoration of a new wine in your marriage. This will bring us to discuss how you must engage in praying heartfelt and honest prayers in alignment with God's will.

Heartfelt, Honest Prayers to Aligned with God's Will

Heartfelt, honest prayers encourage real connection and submission to God's direction. Sincere prayers promote a greater level of faith in God's knowledge and purposes, when it is in line with His will. An essential component of aligning ourselves with God's plans is demonstrating intimacy and trust with Him through heartfelt, honest prayers that expresses our actual needs, wants and emotions.

Here are several ways that heartfelt, honest prayers help us align with God's will:

It strengthens bond and trust: An honest prayer is a powerful way to establish a connection with God, who wants a relationship with us. We present our all before Him in prayer when we pray with the whole of our heart, which builds our faith to receive from Him. Even if His will differs from ours, this confidence makes us more receptive to it making it easy for us to bend to His will without any ounce of doubt.

Refined Intentions and Desires: Heartfelt, honest prayers enable us to reflect on our own motives and hearts. Our aspirations are often reshaped or aligned when we present them to God, becoming more in line with the virtues of love, patience, and humility that characterize His true nature.

Ask for God's Direction: By praying with utmost sincerity and honesty, we ask God to show us His will. In some cases, this can mean that our goals are fulfilled; in other cases, God might gently lead us toward His intentions for us, which are ultimately for our benefit and helps us grow tremendously.

It Fosters Acceptance and Surrender: When we pray honestly, we are practicing the attitude of acceptance and surrender. Jesus' prayer, *"Not my will, but Yours be done,"* in the Garden of Gethsemane in a prayer of total surrender and acceptance that the will of the Father be done. We align ourselves with God's purpose and have faith that He knows what's best for us when we are receptive to His will while being honest about our wants.

It Makes Room for Transformation: Sincere and heartfelt prayer has the power to transform us over time. We discover that God's responses change our own plans so that we see things more as He does, leading us to a deeper knowledge, serenity, or purpose we hadn't anticipated.

Essentially, heartfelt, honest prayer that is accompanied by an open mind to God's responses, no matter how they may come, is in accordance with His will. We allow God to operate in us rather than merely around us when we pray honestly, which strengthens our bond with Him and brings us closer to His purposes. Having been exposed to the reasons and the need for heartfelt, honest prayers in aligning to God's will, this will take us to the next line of action in standing for your marriage.

How to FAST Effectively for Your Marriage

Fasting may be a life-changing exercise, especially if it is done for a specific reason, such as preserving and strengthening your marriage. However, it is a spiritual journey that brings God into the center of a Christian marriage; it goes beyond just avoiding food or luxuries. Intentional fasting is a potent tool for seeking God's direction, removing obstacles, and restoring peace. Whether you're looking for advice for the future or healing from past traumas, understanding how to fast effectively for your marriage results in amazing breakthroughs, hence it is essential. In order to make your fasting journey productive and help you grow closer to God and one another as you work towards a faith-based marriage, we'll go over important procedures and how to fast effectively for your marriage in this chapter.

Set intentions as a team.

Couples must first establish their objectives right if they want to fast effectively in order to succeed in repairing their marriage. Unity and concentration are fostered by talking about your intentions as a team, whether it's forgiveness, a better understanding, or the healing of past hurts. Amos 3:3 asks us, *"How can two walk together unless they have agreed to do so?"* Hence, couples must set objectives together before embarking on a fast, you must align with each other and God.

Choose the Appropriate Time and Duration for the Fast

It's crucial for couples to choose a time that works for them both while preparing to fast. It is not necessary to fast for a lengthy time; a day or a few hours of fasting and prayer may have a significant spiritual impact.

The Bible provides accounts of a variety of fasts, includingJesus' 40-day fast in the desert (Matthew 4:2) and Daniel's

21-day fast (Daniel 10:2-3). The kind of fast and how long it lasts should be carefully considered by couples in light of their commitments, lifestyle, and health. Some people may find that fasting from food is appropriate, while others may decide to abstain from social media or television in order to have more time to devote to God and one another.

Pray together daily

Couples who regularly fast and pray together are more united, have more trust, and are reminded of their dedication to God and one another. Couples' express appreciation, share their joys and worries and rely on God's grace together by fasting together.

In order to build a pattern that deepens their relationship, couples may decide to pray together at certain times of the day. Partners might alternate speaking during prayer so that each one's voice is heard. By increasing emotional closeness, this shared vulnerability provides space for a fresh feeling of trust and love.

Forgive and Let go

Couples may discuss their problems, pains, and miscommunications and beg for forgiveness during fasting and prayer. The significance of forgiveness as a means of healing is emphasized throughout the Bible. As Colossians 3:13 tells us, Colossians 3:13 reminds us, "Bear with each other and forgive one another if any of you has a grievance against someone. Couples may achieve true reconciliation by letting go of previous wounds, which releases them from the weight of anger and animosity.

Even though it might be difficult, couples can use this time to seek God to soften their hearts and help them to forgive. God operates in our hearts when they make a commitment to seek forgiveness together through fasting even though it is a gradual process.

Exercise Self-reflection and Repentance

Fasting promotes humility, which makes it the perfect period for introspection and confession. Each couple can consider how their actions, attitudes, and contributions to their marital problems have affected the marriage while fasting. The Psalmist in Psalms 139:23–24 says "Search me, God, and know my heart; test me and know my anxious thoughts. See if there is any offensive way in me and lead me in the way everlasting. "A good relationship requires personal responsibility, which is fostered by asking God to show them where they need to improve.

Couples have the chance to lay their own hardships and shortcomings before God their hearts are better equipped to show empathy and understanding to one another.

Ask the Holy Spirit to step in and take the Lead

As our comforter and counselor, the Holy Spirit's presence is crucial to the process of marital healing. When fasting together, couples must ask the Holy Spirit to guide their discussions, soften their hearts, and infuse their words and deeds with insight.

Couples who fast experience an increase in spiritual awareness that makes it easier for them to hear the Holy Spirit's gentle prods. As their awareness of His presence grows, they will discover fresh insights, and find answers to their marital problems.

Affirms Love and Fosters Gratitude

Couples may practice gratitude by remembering their benefits and the love that drew them together via effective fasting. According to Philippians 4:6, Christians should offer their petitions to God "with thanksgiving." A spirit of appreciation and love is fostered when couples give thanks to God for one another and the ways He is working in their marriage.

When couples fast, it enables them to take some time to express gratitude to one another for support, compassion, and memories shared. Rekindling affection and reminding each partner of their contribution to the marriage may be accomplished with simple affirmations.

Ask for God's will and direction for the future

Last but not least, fasting provides couples the chance to ask God for direction for their lives and marriage which is embedded in the promises of God to us in the scriptures, see Jeremiah 29:11. Couples who fast and pray give up their goals, aspirations, and worries and put their faith in God to lead them to a future that is in accordance with His will.

They might ask God to give them vision and hope at this time by revealing His plan for their marriage. Fasting and praying for His direction allows God to put aspirations in your hearts, providing them with fresh opportunities to develop as a united front and serve Him.

Rebuilding a marriage through prayer and fasting is a path that calls for endurance, dedication, and faith. It is a lovely invitation to entrust your marriage to God and rely on Him to remold, strengthen, and heal it. I encourage couples to engage in prayer and fasting to strengthen their faith, cultivate their love, adopt an attitude of understanding and forgiveness. Couples will reconnect with one another by embracing these activities together, finding a fresh love, resiliency, and joy that mirrors God's plan for marriage.

Prayers points while fasting for your marriage

Dear God,

I know I have made significant mistakes, but I also know that you love me dearly. You created me in your image, and I recognize that I have strayed from that truth. I failed to include you in my relationship and marriage, and I ask for your help in restoring what has been broken. Although my marriage was never strong from the start, I believe in the power of the God I serve. You are capable of healing and restoring, and I know that if I follow your guidance, you can mend my marriage.

I am committing this situation into your hands, where it should have been from the beginning. I am ready to let you take over and do the work that needs to be done. I must admit, however, that I will struggle with worry and doubt along the way. I understand that these feelings can delay the healing process, but I ask that during those moments, you send the Holy Spirit to comfort me. Help me to remember that I don't need to worry or doubt because you have everything under control. I just need to trust in the process, no matter how long it may take.

Lord, I also need your help to examine my heart and understand how I may have contributed to the separation between my spouse and me. I want to hold myself accountable for my actions, so please reveal to me the ways I have fallen short. Once I recognize my mistakes, help me to get back on the right path—not only in my relationship with you but also in my relationship with my husband or wife.

This pain is overwhelming, and I never imagined that my partner would leave. I have always prioritized their needs and desires. So, Lord, I trust you because I have no other choice. Thank you for your forgiveness and for giving me another chance to make things right. I offer this prayer in Jesus' name. Amen.

Chapter 5

The Importance Of Staying Positive

Marriage is a journey filled with moments of joy, companionship, and growth, but it can also face seasons of doubts, pain, disappointment, and brokenness. When a marriage feels fractured or lost, it can be hard to hold on to hope. Many people struggle with feelings of betrayal, loss, and the heavy burden of unmet expectations, leading to a sense of hopelessness. In these dark times, it's natural to question whether healing is even possible. However, what seems impossible in the moment can often be restored with patience, faith, and a commitment to rebuilding.

Have you found yourself questioning the future of your marriage or wondering if the love you once shared can ever return? If so, you are not alone. Many couples face seasons of intense difficulty, but countless stories reveal that restoration is achievable, even in marriages that seemed beyond repair. Yours can be as well! By nurturing hope and faith like we shared earlier, couples can create a foundation for healing that not only mends the wounds of the past but also strengthens the bond for the future.

The transformative power of positivity cannot be overstated in the journey to restore a marriage. Positivity shifts your focus from what is broken to what can be healed. It provides a pathway toward intentionality and restores hope. Positivity encourages couples to keep moving forward, step by step, toward a marriage that is not only restored but renewed.

No marriage is beyond hope when approached with a spirit of faith and a willingness to grow together. While the road may be challenging, the reward of a renewed, resilient marriage is worth the journey. In this chapter we shall be looking at the power of positivity in restoration of marriage.

Guarding Your Heart and Mind from Negativity While Standing for Your Marriage God's Way

"Keep your heart with all diligence; for out of it are the issues of life" (Proverbs 4:23).

When you're working to restore a broken marriage, protecting your heart and mind from negativity is crucial. It's not an easy road, and while you're holding onto hope, it can feel like negativity—both from inside and outside—is waiting at every turn. The feelings of pain, anger, or disappointment you're experiencing are absolutely normal, but letting those emotions take over can make healing seem impossible. At the same time, well-meaning friends, family, or society may offer advice that, while intended to help, might make things feel even harder. By learning to guard your heart and mind, you're creating a healthier space for yourself where real restoration can happen.

Managing Internal Negativity

When a marriage is broken, it's completely natural to feel overwhelmed by sadness, anger, betrayal, or even guilt. These emotions are all part of the healing process. But if they're left unchecked, they can easily turn into a cycle of negativity that blocks out hope. So, what can you do? Start by acknowledging these feelings. They're a part of the journey, and recognizing them rather than pushing them aside can bring a huge sense of relief. But while it's okay to feel this way, letting these emotions take the wheel can make moving forward a lot harder.

One practical way to handle these feelings is by journaling. Writing down what you're experiencing gives you an outlet, letting you process your emotions without letting them build up or take control. It's like having a safe space to get everything out in the open without judgment. Another helpful approach is practicing self-compassion—treating yourself with the same kindness you'd offer a friend going through a tough time. It's a reminder that it's okay to struggle, as long as you don't let that struggle define your outlook. You can also work on reframing negative thoughts into hopeful ones. For instance, instead of thinking, "This is too broken to fix," try, "We're taking steps, and healing is possible." These little shifts may seem small, but over time, they add up, helping you keep a more hopeful perspective.

Handling External Negativity

While managing what's going on internally can be tough, dealing with external negativity can sometimes feel even harder. Family, friends, and sometimes even society can put pressure on you, often without meaning to. They might suggest it's time to move on, or they may be skeptical about the possibility of reconciliation. Even though they may just be trying to help, these messages can feel heavy and disheartening when you're holding onto hope for restoration.

Setting boundaries with people who might unintentionally bring negativity into your life is key. If someone you know tends to be unsupportive, try limiting conversations about your marriage with them. A simple, respectful response like, "I really appreciate your concern, but I'm focused on working toward healing in my marriage," you can let them know where you stand without inviting further opinions. Instead, seek out people or groups who support your journey. Support groups, counselors, or communities that focus on marriage healing can be amazing sources of encouragement and strength. Talking with people who understand what you're going through can make the process feel a little less lonely. I am always here to help as well.

Restoring a marriage takes time, but by guarding your heart and mind, you're giving yourself the best chance at true healing and a renewed, hopeful future together.

Speak life over your marriage and spouse

When a marriage is struggling, it's easy to focus on everything that's wrong or to let hurtful words take over our conversations. But when it comes to restoring a relationship, the words we choose—and the intentions behind them—can make all the difference. Speaking life which is speaking the Word of God and hope over your marriage and your spouse might sound simple, but it's a powerful approach to shift both your mindset and the atmosphere in your relationship. Words can be like seeds, planting hope, peace, and the belief that things can get better. How much more the unfailing power of God's word.

Even when it feels like all hope is lost, speaking words of love and encouragement can create room for healing and help pave the way for restoration.

The Power of Words in Shifting Mindset

When things feel broken, it's natural for our thoughts and words to reflect the frustration and pain we're feeling. You might feel stuck thinking, "This will never change," or "We're just too far gone." But words have an incredible way of shaping our mindset, whether positively or negatively. Choosing words that focus on hope and healing, rather than frustration or disappointment, can start to shift how you see your marriage—and how your spouse does too.

Imagine what a difference it could make if, instead of dwelling on the difficulties, you focused on small words of affirmation each day. This doesn't mean ignoring what's hard or pretending things are fine. It's about intentionally making room for hope and possibility. Try saying simple phrases like, "I believe we're working towards something better," or "Our marriage can heal and grow stronger." Over time, these small words can have a big impact. They open up your heart to the idea that, while things are tough now, they don't have to stay that way.

Choosing Words of Hope and Encouragement

When in a struggling marriage, it can feel awkward or look like you're being forced to say positive things, especially when things seem anything but hopeful. But even if it feels strange at first, small words of encouragement can build a foundation of trust and connection. All through the book of Proverbs, we are told that the power of life and death resides in our spoken words. Proverbs 4: 20-22. Try offering simple, honest affirmations that remind both you and your spouse of the possibility of a brighter future.

Start small and straightforward: "I'm hopeful for our future," or "I'm grateful for the progress we're making." Or try focusing on specific positive traits about your spouse, even if things are tense. You might say, "I appreciate your patience with me," or "I see the effort you're making, and it means a lot." These kinds of words are genuine, and they don't ignore the challenges you're facing. Instead, they help shift the focus toward small, positive steps, which can build up over time. In moments of doubt, these words of encouragement are like reminders that healing is a journey—and one that's worth believing in.

The Role of Prayer and Affirmations

In addition to speaking encouraging words to your spouse, using affirmations and prayer can be powerful tools for changing how you see your marriage. Positive affirmations and prayers focused on love, healing, and forgiveness help strengthen your commitment to the relationship. Think of these affirmations as a way of grounding yourself in your goals and beliefs for your marriage. Just as you might remind yourself of the importance of patience or resilience, affirming your desire for healing can strengthen your sense of purpose on hard days.

Try saying affirmations each day, even if it's just to yourself. Phrases like, "I believe our marriage can be **healed, "or** "I'm open to new beginnings with my spouse," can plant seeds of hope in your heart and mind. These affirmations may feel simple, but repeating them daily can help you stay focused on what you're working toward. And if you're comfortable, include your spouse in these affirmations. Saying them together, or even just saying them out loud when they're around, can show that you're committed to the journey of restoration.

Prayer, too, can be an anchor. Pray for your marriage, for healing, and for a renewed love between you and your spouse. You might pray for patience, for understanding, and for the wisdom to know how to move forward. Simple prayers like, "God, please help us heal and find peace in each **other,** or "Help me speak love and hope into our marriage," can bring calm and purpose, helping you remember that you're not alone in this journey.

Daily Repetition and Faith-Based Declarations

Consistency is key when it comes to speaking life over your marriage. Repeating words of hope and faith-based affirmations daily helps solidify your commitment and trains your mind to see possibilities instead of just problems. Think of it as building a habit—each day, you're choosing to invest in your marriage by speaking life into it, even if you don't see immediate results.

Try setting a daily routine to remind yourself of these affirmations and prayers, maybe in the morning or before bed just like how we use drugs prescriptions. The Word of God teaches us that we bind them continually in our hearts and that we should not let them depart out of our mouth. Over time, these small steps add up, creating a positive foundation for the road ahead. On days when things feel especially tough, lean into these words. Let them remind you why you're committed to this journey of healing and restoration.

In the end, speaking life and hope over your marriage isn't just about your words—it's about believing in the possibility of healing. Each word of encouragement, every affirmation, and each prayer helps you stay focused on a future where your marriage is renewed. The power of speaking **life-giving** words from the scriptures is that it opens up space for restoration, one word, one day, at a time. Be reminded that the Word of God has the creative ability to make things brand new, your marriage inclusive.

Start declaring now! Say something good to your marriage!

Would you?

Identifying and Challenging Negative Thoughts

Negative thoughts are normal, especially when you're dealing with the rebuilding of a marriage. It's common to feel frustration, anger, or even hopelessness, but getting stuck in these feelings can be exhausting. The key is to notice when you're slipping into patterns of despair or anger so that you can challenge these thoughts before they take root. The Word of God calls it "guarding your heart with all diligence" because "we are not ignorant of the devices of the enemy."

One helpful technique is reframing. When a negative thought crosses your mind, try rephrasing it in a way that allows room for hope or growth. For example, instead of thinking, "We'll never get through this," try, "We're facing challenges, but we're working toward something better." It may feel a bit forced at first, but with practice, reframing can change your perspective.

Another great tool is gratitude journaling. Each day, write down a few things you're grateful for, even if they seem small or unrelated to your marriage. Gratitude journaling reminds you that even during hard times, there are still positives to focus on. You might find yourself more appreciative of small gestures from your spouse or start noticing progress in areas you hadn't before. It's with joy that you can draw from the wells of salvation and the best way to ignite your joy is to stay grateful.

Also, the **Holy Spirit** is our present help, friend and comforter. Rely on Him daily for discernment to filter thoughts that aren't in consistency with the promises God has made to you concerning your marriage. When He does prompt you on these negative thoughts, ask Him for grace not to feed on them. Rather replace them with the truth of God's word.

Minimizing Exposure to Negative Influences

Sometimes, staying positive also means being mindful of what you're **allowing** into your mind and heart. Friends, family, and even certain media can unknowingly contribute to negativity. For instance, if someone close to you is unsupportive of your efforts to restore your marriage, their words may add to your frustration or doubts. It doesn't mean you have to cut people off, but setting boundaries can help you create space to focus on your own goals without outside opinions pulling you down.

Consider surrounding yourself with positive influences instead. This might mean watching or reading things that uplift and encourage you, or joining a **Christian** support group where you can share your struggles in a constructive, hopeful environment. Marriage counseling programs can also be incredibly helpful. Professional counselors can offer guidance that is tailored to your situation, helping you and your spouse work through specific issues without the added stress of unhelpful outside voices. Additionally, consuming positive media—podcasts, books, or videos focused on healing and restoration—can shift your focus to stories and ideas that inspire rather than discourage you. Above all, make the Scriptures your meditation. Eat the Word and make it your weapon of war against the demon fighting your marriage. It's your tool for resisting the enemy and to make him flee from you and your marriage completely.

One very sure way to minimize negative exposure and influences, is to meditate on God's Word, day in, day out (Joshua 1:8).

Creating a Support System

A strong support system can be one of the most powerful assets in staying positive. Finding people who understand and support your goal of restoring your marriage can give you the encouragement you need on tough days. Accountability partners, mentors, or even friends who have been through similar experiences can offer practical advice and a sense of camaraderie.

If possible, try finding someone who has experienced restoration in their own marriage. They'll have a unique understanding of the struggles you're facing and can offer both empathy and wisdom from personal experience. Knowing someone who has come out the other side of a similar situation can remind you that healing is possible, even when it feels distant. They can serve as a reminder that setbacks don't have to define the journey and that progress can often look like small, consistent steps forward.

Prayer Points for Guarding your hearts

1. "Heavenly Father, I ask that You fill my heart with hope and positivity as I wait for the restoration of my marriage. It's so easy to focus on what's broken and feel discouraged, but I know that You are a God of miracles and new beginnings. Remind me daily of Your promises and keep my eyes on You. Help me to speak words of life and love over my marriage,

even when I feel weary. Let hope be my anchor, and may I find joy in each small step forward. Amen."

2. "Father God, I ask for Your strength as I work to stay positive in this challenging season. There are days when it feels impossible to hold onto hope, but I know that You are my source of strength. Help me to stay focused on Your goodness, to remember Your faithfulness, and to believe that better days are coming. When I am weak, lift me up, and when I am discouraged, remind me of Your love. Fill my heart with courage and positivity, even when the path forward seems unclear. Amen."

3. "Lord, as I wait on You, work within my heart and mind. Transform any negativity into hope and any doubt into faith. Renew my spirit so that I can see my marriage through Your eyes, full of potential and promise. Help me to be a source of encouragement and love for my spouse, reflecting the peace and positivity You give me. Make me a vessel of Your love and grace, and let my words and actions be filled with kindness and hope. Amen."

4. "Lord, thank You for the blessings that I have, even in this season of waiting. Teach me to look for the positives each day, to see glimpses of Your work, and to appreciate the small signs of progress. Help me to be grateful for the ways You are shaping and

refining me, and let my gratitude fuel my positivity. May I learn to see my marriage with hope, trusting that You are bringing restoration in ways I cannot yet see. Thank You for Your endless love and patience. Amen."

As we gradually draw the curtains to this chapter, I would like to remind you that Marriage restoration is challenging, and staying positive isn't about ignoring the difficulties but about keeping your focus on the hope of a better future. By recognizing and reframing negative thoughts, carefully selecting the influences around you, and building a support system, you're giving yourself the best possible foundation to keep moving forward. In the end, surrounding yourself with positivity and support can make all the difference in helping you find strength, even on the hardest days. Remember to actually make the Holy Spirit your friend and comforter in these challenging times. Draw strength from Him and constantly renew your mind with the Word of God. I am confident that this will end in praise!

Chapter 6

The Power Of Support Systems

Is there someone you can talk to when there are issues in your marriage? Are there people of you can run to when it seems like the devil is gaining ground in your marriage? I guess this question rings a bell in your mind, right? We all need a good support system; don't you think so?

Support systems are a strong force in life, offering a basis that helps people overcome obstacles, develop individuals, and accomplish their objectives. More than simply companions, these networks of spouse, friends, family, mentors, and coworkers provide support, resources, direction, and strength, boosting resilience and promoting general well-being. It is impossible to overestimate the importance of having a solid support network in the modern world, when stress and uncertainty are prevalent.

The emotional fortitude that a support system gives is among its most important advantages. Having someone to turn to during difficult times, such as a health problem, marital troubles, or a job loss, makes the situation much less solitary. It serves as a reminder that you're not alone in your troubles. The power of a support system is vital for helping people overcome adversity. Social support has a good effect on mental health and has been shown to reduce rates of anxiety, depression, and even suicide.

In addition, support systems act as partners in accountability and as motivators. Setting and achieving objectives, including getting a degree, launching a company, or changing to healthy habits, may be difficult, particularly when there are setbacks. When motivation wanes, supportive people— spouses, friends, mentors, or coworkers—can inspire tenacity, provide insightful counsel and remind you of the wider picture. Having someone to answer to encourages spouses to stick with their objectives because they know that someone else cares about their success.

Moreover, support systems provide useful information and assistance that may really aid you during difficult times. For example, friends or relatives may give money or provide temporary housing during a financial crisis. In the event that someone has a personal emergency, coworkers may cover work duties. In times of disaster, communities often come together to organize resources and provide aid to people in need. By relieving responsibilities and assisting people in regaining stability, these material kinds of assistance have the power to transform lives.

The knowledge and direction that support systems provide is another important power it wields. Having access to competent and reliable people change lives, whether via spouses, mentors, instructors, or just those with greater experience. Advice from those who have "been there" gives you perspective and offers tactics and insights that may help you save time, prevent errors, and improve your chances of success.

Furthermore, having a support system has a good impact on both the individual receiving help and the individual rendering it. Supporting others increases empathy, creates a feeling of purpose, and fortifies ties within the network. According to research, assisting others causes the release of feel-good chemicals like dopamine, which leads to a sensation of contentment and fulfillment.

Understanding the value of support networks serves as a reminder that, despite the tendency toward autonomy in our society, we are all interconnected. A strong support system enables individuals to develop in ways they couldn't on their own, deal with obstacles more skillfully, and weather life's ups and downs with optimism and perseverance. By making an investment in and maintaining these relationships, people and communities build a strong foundation that will be beneficial to all.

Building a Network of Godly Support during Difficult Times

During challenging times in a marriage, establishing a network of godly support provides strength, knowledge, and encouragement. The scriptures also support couples who seeks wise advice, relies on each other, and pray together in line with your desire to surround yourself with godly mentors, friends, and family who are spiritually mature will be a huge source of support for you. The scriptures also gave workable strategies for building a network of godly support in these challenging times:

Look for Mentors Who Exhibit the Love of Christ

Look for a mentor with a solid foundation in God's Word and a strong marriage that provides priceless insight and direction. If possible, this mentor should value your connection with your spouse and promote harmony rather than conflict.

Proverbs 11:14 – "Where there is no guidance, a people falls, but in an abundance of counselors there is safety."

Seek for mentors you have so much respect for and who have a strong spiritual foundation; they will provide you with godly counsels, spiritual and real-life experience they've garnered as a result of their long years of experience in keeping their marriage godly and fulfilling God's mandate in their home to help you work through marital challenges.

Establish Connections with Other Believers

Prayer, support, and encouragement can be obtained from close friends who share your beliefs. Prioritize developing friendships with people who share your commitment to upholding God in all of your interactions. In trying times, these people can encourage you, pray for you, and remind you of God's promises to see you through.

Ecclesiastes 4:9-10 – "Two are better than one, because they have a good return for their labor: If either of them falls down, one can help the other up."

When we find it difficult to see beyond the present and future, godly networks provide us with courage and hope to scale through.

Be Receptive to Support from your Church

Be willing to accept help from your church community. Church communities often provide couples with organized assistance through Bible study, marital counseling, and small groups. One excellent method to learn from other Christian couples who have gone through similar problems is to take part in marital enrichment courses or join a small group for married couples.

Hebrews 10:24-25 – "And let us consider how to stir up one another to love and good works, not neglecting to meet together, as is the habit of some, but encouraging one another…"

Attending church regularly gives couples a safe space to talk, pray, and support one another in upholding moral values and restoring their marriage.

Seek Prayers from trusted Believers

Prayer is a powerful tool, and asking people to pray for you encourages and supports you spiritually. Look for dependable Christians who will diligently bring your troubles before God while keeping your issues private because the prayer of the saints is powerful and effective.

James 5:16 – "Therefore, confess your sins to each other and pray for each other so that you may be healed. The prayer of a righteous person is powerful and effective."

In addition to offering consolation and support, a network of godly prayer provides opportunities for God to step in and lead your marriage.

Communicate Openly and Honestly with Your Support System

To get the appropriate support you require, one must be honest. Those who are trustworthy and spiritually mature provide precise advice and pray more specifically when you honestly discuss your concerns with them. Just as the scriptures says:

Proverbs 27:17 – "Iron sharpens iron, and one person sharpens another."

When we are open with others, they are better able to sharpen us with truth, love, and encouragement.

People are better equipped to hone us with love, truth, and support when we are honest with them.

Encourage an Attitude of Accountability and Humility

Only when we approach a support system with humility and remain receptive to guidance and criticism will it be helpful. Even when it's hard to hear, those with a modest heart will communicate the right advice to us.

Proverbs 12:15 – "The way of fools seems right to them, but the wise listen to advice."

Ask for input, be open to making adjustments, and let other people assist you in upholding moral standards.

Unite in prayer Often

God is ultimately the cornerstone of every effective support system. God is invited to work in your relationship when you pray together, whether it's with your spouse, mentor, or church members. Involve God in every aspect of your life, understanding that His presence restores your marriage and gives your network the ability to encourage and assist you.

Creating a Godly support system entails consciously looking for individuals who respect the sanctity of marriage, love God, and are prepared to help you throughout trying times. You must create a support system that is in line with biblical principles and enables you to weather marital storms with faith and fortitude if you engage in prayer, humble ourselves and practice consistency.

The Importance of Surrounding Yourself with Positive, Faith-filled People

It's crucial to surround oneself with uplifting, faith-filled individuals in your marriage because they provide support, guidance, and encouragement based on love and faith. A network of these people is very helpful to couples in overcoming obstacles, strengthening their bond and being faithful to God's plan for their union. I will be sharing the importance of surrounding yourself with positive faith-filled people in a moment, just stay with me.

They Encourage Spiritual Development and Responsibility

Faith-based friends provide accountability that promotes spiritual development for both spouses. They serve to maintain Christ at the heart of the relationship by serving as a constant reminder to prioritize prayer, the word of God and moral values. Accountability is quite helpful, particularly in stressful or conflicting situations.

Both spouses are more likely to develop spiritual maturity when they are surrounded with those who encourage them to seek a closer connection with God. Faith-filled people challenge us to exhibit Godly character, humility, and love in our marriages, helping to "sharpen" one another.

They Offer Support When Things Get Tough

There are highs and lows in marriage. It's easy to feel overburdened when couples have difficulties, whether they be related to money, health, sex or relationships. Encouragement comes from positive, devout individuals who share their own challenges, remind couples of God's promises, and provide hope when things seem hopeless. Couples will be able to overcome obstacles together with the support of their faith-filled friends or family, which builds resilience in them.

When you're surrounded with the company of faith-filled people, you receive encouragement to persevere during difficult circumstances by reminding us of God's faithfulness.

They Provide Astute, Bible-Based Advice

Faith-filled friends provide us with biblical insight and helpful counsel that helps us deal with challenging circumstances in a loving, understanding, and patient manner. They advise us to handle disagreements with compassion, respect and to react with love rather than anger. Making informed judgments that are consistent with God's Word requires having individuals who are firmly rooted in faith and well-versed in the word. Wise counsel is vital in marriage. In tough circumstances, couples begin to discover answers and strengthen their bond with the support of wise counsel from friends who are positive minded and faith-filled.

They Foster Love and Unity

Positive minded and faith-filled friends foster love and unity in marriage. It might be easy to turn to friends when a couple is having problems, but doing so may unintentionally promote unfavorable attitudes or behaviors that undermine the couple's togetherness. However, those who are Godly place a higher value on togetherness, love, and reconciliation. They will support spouses in seeking a solution, keeping their word and communicating with love. They serve as a reminder of the sanctity of marriage, strengthening couple's will to stay together and assisting them in overcoming obstacles in a morally upright manner. Friends who are faith-filed promote harmony and tranquility, which helps couples become closer and resolve disputes amicably.

They help in Building a Robust Prayer Support System

The power of having people prays for you and your marriage is amazing. Faith-filled friends know the importance of prayer and will pray with you as well as for you, strengthening your marriage throughout trying times. The spiritual foundation that prayer builds allows God's knowledge, healing, and presence to dwell in a marriage. When faith-filled friends offer prayers over a marriage, they are standing with the couple in the hope that God may bless, strengthen, and restore their union. A strong support network based on God's love is provided by the consolation, encouragement, and strength that come from prayer from those who are faith-filled.

They Create Lasting Company that Show the Love of Christ

Marriage is meant to be a reflection of God's love, and it is both uplifting and humbling to have faith-filled friends who embody the love that God intended for marriages to represent. These friends serve as a model for living a life that glorifies God, serving as a reminder of the value of love, forgiveness and humility. Regularly spending time with other Christian couples allows couples to exchange ideas, learn from one another's experiences, and be inspired by similar ideals and beliefs. Couples are encouraged to treat one another with patience, compassion, and humility when they are with others who exhibit Christ's love, which strengthens their marriage.

They Create an Environment Focused on Christ

Positive, faith-filled individuals contribute to the development of an atmosphere that upholds Godly principles. When the opinions around a marriage emphasize holiness, it is simpler to embody such principles inside the marriage.

This setting encourages both spouses to align their thoughts and actions with God's desire because it reminds them of God's love and aligns their faith. Being surrounded by others who share similar ideals keeps us focused on God and fosters harmony and happiness in our marriage.

Without any doubt, you can see that when you surround yourself with positive and faith-filled individuals, you enjoy vital attributes to a marriage. They set examples of Godly ideas, offer insight, accountability, and support. Their influence helps couples in becoming closer, overcoming obstacles, and keeping God at the center of their marriage. In the end, having this kind of support network will be life-changing, resulting in a marriage that not only survives hardships but flourishes because of love, faith, unity as well as you keeping the company of positive and faith-filled friends.

How To Choose the Right People to Confide in And Avoid Negativity

Now that you have the understanding and importance of surrounding yourself with positive and faith-filled people, you have to pray and ask God to send the right people to your life to help you. You have to pray because the onus is on you to choose the right circle of people to confide in to preserve your marriage.

As much as we should be careful doing this, building good connections, avoiding negativity, and choosing the right individuals to confide in are all crucial for spiritual growth, emotional health and personal development. Selecting the right individuals may have a big impact on how we respond to life's obstacles because they have a huge impact on our opinions, attitudes, and choices. I'll be sharing with you some guidelines to assist you in choosing trustworthy, confidants while steering clear of those that might add negativity to your life.

Evaluate their Values and Character.

Evaluating the character and values of the people you want to confide in is one of the most important ways to prevent negativity in your marriage. You may be confident that the counsel you get will be in line with your own ideals if you choose someone who shares your values and faith-based principles. Choose people who exhibit honesty, compassion, and decency. These traits make people less likely to breach your confidence and more likely to handle sensitive information with care.

Confidentiality and trust are essential; entrusting someone who divulges your personal information or thoughts without your perception may cause miscommunications, strain relationships, and undermine trust. A friend who constantly spreads rumors about other people, for instance, would not be the ideal person to confide in. Instead, look for individuals that have a reputation for caution and have shown respect for privacy.

Seek for optimistic, problem-solving thinkers.

It's crucial to look for confidants who are steadfast in faith and focused on finding solutions rather than those who are obsessed over issues without providing helpful advice. Negative thoughts could inadvertently increase your worries, adding unnecessary stress to an already challenging circumstance. However, positive, encouraging persons will boost your spirits, help you see the wider picture, and gently lead you toward answers without making you feel less of yourself. You will be encouraged and given a positive perspective on issues by confiding in someone who has a growth mentality and sees the potential. A resilient and optimistic person, for example, might assist you in seeing a setback as a chance for development rather than a loss.

Make Emotional Stability and Maturity a Priority.

Your sense of support may be greatly improved by confiding in emotionally secure and mature people. People that are emotionally stable tend to be more empathetic, patient, and less prone to react without impulse nor judgmental in nature. Because of their maturity, they are able to listen to you without imposing their own problems on your circumstances and provide fair, unbiased counsel. Selecting confidants who maintain composure under pressure also assist you in keeping your own emotions in check and improve your decision-making. Family members, friends, or mentors who are emotionally mature provide a secure environment where you can be vulnerable without worrying about being rejected or subjected to severe criticism.

Be on the Lookout for people who respect boundaries and are supportive.

Good confidants have regard for boundaries but yours and theirs. They won't force you to make choices or encroach on topics you aren't ready to talk about. Rather, they provide assistance according to your preferences, letting you steer the discussion at your own pace. Make sure they are individuals who are attentive to the fact that everyone has varying degrees of comfort with vulnerability. Boundaries must be respected in order to prevent feeling overburdened or pressured to make quick judgments. Furthermore, honoring limits is reciprocal; in order to avoid unintentionally overtaxing people, it's critical to be aware of their own limitations and emotional capacity.

Steer clear of toxic patterns and negative influences

Recognizing favorable traits is crucial, but it's also critical to see warning signs in those who might negatively impact your life. This might include those who are always negative, have a propensity to control others, or are very pessimistic in nature. Confiding in someone who exhibits toxic habits like envy, gossip, or a lack of responsibility may be emotionally taxing and even harmful to you and your spouse.

You can avoid the trap of confiding in others who could reject your sentiments, pass judgment harshly, or impede your own development by being conscious of similar behaviors in other people. Though prolonged negativity often hinders rather than helps, keep in mind that constructive criticism is also beneficial.

Consider Previous Experiences and have Trust Your Intuition

Sometimes prior experiences are the greatest way to choose who to confide in. You can determine if someone is trustworthy and helpful by thinking back on how they have handled sensitive information or advice in the past. Someone could be a good option if they have previously honored your emotions, given you sound advice, and kept your trust unbroken. But when it comes to delicate issues, it's preferable to avoid them if they've not been trustworthy.

Furthermore, trust your gut, since our instincts often provide information that logical evaluations can miss. It could be wiser to heed your instincts and seek assistance elsewhere if you are uncomfortable or reluctant to confide in someone.

Build a Trusting Circle

Consider creating a small group of dependable friends, mentors, or family members with a range of skills and viewpoints rather than depending too much on one or two individuals. You'll gain from a variety of experiences and perspectives, as each individual provides unique insights or emotional support. In addition to offering more thorough and balanced assistance, a well-rounded support system will assist you in avoiding overwhelming anyone with your worries.

Different individuals may be more equipped to assist you with different kinds of problems, whether they be spiritual, professional, or personal, and you will get counsel that is particular to different areas of your life.

You must carefully evaluate the stability, values, and character of the people you surround yourself with in order to choose the correct individuals to confide in and stay away from negativity. Confidants benefit greatly from the presence of faith-filled individuals who respect boundaries, are emotionally mature, and foster personal development. You safeguard your mental health and create a supportive atmosphere that promotes resilience and happiness by intentionally creating a supporting network for yourself and your spouse. By staying away from bad influences, you may confide in a manner that is secure, growth-oriented, and productive, which eventually helps you make choices and deal with difficulties clearly and with clarity.

Prayer points for God to bring good people your way

Oh Lord my God, I thank you for I know that You possess all power in heaven and on earth to secure my marriage. Lord Jesus, I pray for Your wisdom stand direction that will help me and my spouse surround ourselves with the appropriate individuals who will encourage, elevate, and fortify us in our commitment, love, and faith.

Surround us with faith-filled individuals who will encourage us to become closer to You and that will continue to remind us of our commitments. Lord Jesus, lead us towards harmony, understanding, forgiveness, love and shield us from any influence that can wreak havoc in our marriage. May Your love continue to serve as the cornerstone of our marriage and help us to retain You at its core, in the name of Jesus, Amen.

Chapter 7

Keeping Busy- Preventing The Enemy'S Lies

It is simpler than ever to succumb to pessimism, self-doubt, and even dangerous thoughts in today's fast-paced, digitalized society where we have access to quick gratification and a plethora of distractions.

These "enemies," whether they are negative self-talk, self-destructive behaviors, or external influences, can distort reality and undermine our sense of purpose, and self-worth. These lies often infiltrate covertly, weakening mental toughness, fostering anxiety and insecurity.

To combat these damaging forces, there is a straightforward yet effective way to go about it: Keeping busy- Preventing the Enemy's Lies. By investing time and effort into worthwhile endeavors, one can strengthen oneself against the damaging effects of these critical voices and cultivate a more positive and healthier mindset.

In Proverbs "an idle mind is the devil's playground" reminds us of the perils of mental inertia. The mind becomes more vulnerable to forces that could lead it in a darker direction when it is left idle or allowed to focus on unimportant or unfavorable topics and thoughts. These times of inactivity are when doubts, anxieties, and uncertainties are most prone to creep into our minds and expose us to the "enemy's" sneaky whispers.

However, when one's time is occupied with constructive pursuits, a natural barrier against negative thoughts is established. Whether it's by taking up new hobbies, learning new skills, or participating in social events, being active and purposefully occupied is an intentional attempt to promote resilience, mental clarity, and purpose rather than just killing time.

In this chapter, I'll focus on how couples can avoid distractions, stay active all the time, deal with the enemy by keeping busy, the nature of the enemies lies so you won't become a victim and how to keep your focus on God alone amongst others.

The Nature of "Enemy's Lies"

The first step in comprehending why keeping busy is such a successful tactic is to determine what the "enemy's lies" are. Although these falsehoods may take many various shapes based on a person's background, personality, and surroundings, they often center on the same themes: pessimism, fear, self-doubt, and worthlessness. People who are battling with previous failures, for example, may be plagued by notions that they will never succeed, and people who are lonely may start to feel that they are not deserving of love or friendship. Such falsehoods lead to a vicious cycle in which one's emotional and mental health suffers as bad thoughts fuel more negativity.

It is also possible to see this "enemy" as a confluence of external and internal forces. These are the internalized prejudices and restrictive views we have about ourselves, often stemming from trauma, failures, or prior experiences.

Toxic relationships, media influence, or social expectations that impose unreasonable standards are some examples of external manifestations of the adversary. When combined, these factors have the power to warp our perspective, impairing our judgment and causing us to base judgments more on fear or uncertainty than on our confidence in God. In times of weakness, the adversary flourishes, particularly when the mind is unoccupied and susceptible to suggestion, fabricating falsehoods that may lead to a downward spiral. Staying active consistently is the only solution out of the enemy's lies. Keeping busy will help couples to stay focused and standing for their marriage and making room for God to have His way.

How do I Refuse to Despair and Stay Active?

Although relationships are very fulfilling, maintaining the mental health and happiness of both parties often calls for constant work and care. Maintaining a healthy emotional and physical relationship helps couples remain balanced, connected, and fulfilled. Without these common interests and hobbies, it's simple for couples to get into depressing cycles where they feel like their marriage is stalling or to engage in obsessive behaviors where they put too much pressure on one another. In order to maintain a strong and thriving marriage, couples must build a foundation of mutual support and shared purpose by encouraging active, thoughtful, and balanced habits.

Couples can remain active together in a number of ways to strengthen their marriage, keep a good outlook, and steer clear of the dangers of hopelessness or compulsive attachment as well as avoid falling into despair or obsession over the situation. The following I am about to discuss are strategies couples can engage to stay active and steer clear of depression.

Encourage Physical Activities and Common Interests

Please note this if you are a couple. The easiest, but most effective, method for couples to stay active is to discover a physical activity or interest they both like. Sports, dancing, swimming, hiking, and other physical activities provide people a chance to connect, talk, and even push one another. Exercise is known to produce endorphins, which can elevate mood and lower stress levels, allowing couples to enjoy each other's company without feeling burdened by everyday obligations. The mutual satisfaction of a satisfying exercise or enjoyable game can increase self-esteem and foster favorable relationships.

Exercise doesn't have to be the only shared activity. Cooking, drawing, and gardening are examples of creative ways that are very effective to strengthen marriages. In addition to keeping the mind active, working on a project together can be very fulfilling, particularly when couples see the fruits of their labor. These encounters leave a lasting impression and contribute to the development of a repertoire of shared experiences that gradually strengthen the bond between the two parties.

- ***Be Independent***

In addition to strengthening a couple's bond via common hobbies, it's critical for each partner to pursue their own passions. The relationship may avoid being obsessive, when one person's identity and self-worth become too reliant on the other, by maintaining personal independence. Engaging in personal interests, pursuing professional objectives, or spending time with friends and family allows couples to contribute fresh perspectives, experiences, and anecdotes to the marriage.

In a marriage, this independence encourages mutual respect, appreciation, and interest. Couples tend to avoid the "claustrophobic" sensation that can sometimes occur in marriages when partners become too dependent on one another for every element of their enjoyment by preserving their uniqueness.

As both spouses continue to develop on their own, autonomy helps avoid emotional stagnation and maintains a dynamic and interesting marriage.

- ***Make Honesty and Open Communication a Priority***

Misunderstandings or unfulfilled expectations in marriage are often the root cause of despair and obsession. To resolve any worries or annoyances before they become more serious problems, open communication is crucial. Regular check-ins between spouses create a healthy environment where both parties feel respected and heard.

Whether it's a weekly check-in or a quick chat at the end of the day, it's helpful to schedule time expressly for candid chats. These conversations should provide each partner the chance to speak about their emotions, ideas, and any areas in which they may need help. This practice of open conversation promotes emotional transparency, which helps shield against negative cycles that might result in hopelessness or an obsession with each other for comfort and stop resentments from accumulating.

- ***Set and Pursue Goals Together***

Couples can avoid emotions of hopelessness and stagnation by establishing shared objectives that provide them a sense of purpose and direction. These objectives may pertain to personal growth, travel, health, or finances. Collaborating to achieve common goals strengthens the relationship and promotes support between couples because it reinforces the sense that both parties are on the same team.

For instance, a couple may choose to train for a marathon, collaborate on a home renovation project, or save for a trip. Beyond the daily chores, they develop a feeling of togetherness and achievement as they go forward together. In addition to avoiding the traps of fixation by focusing energy on worthwhile and satisfying endeavors, having long-term objectives to strive for helps lower the likelihood of despair by giving the marriage a forward-looking perspective.

- ***Continue to Engage in Physical Activity Together***

In addition to its health advantages, physical exercise is a great way for people to bond and become more intimate. Couples who exercise together, whether it's stretching in the morning, attending a dancing class, or jogging, enjoy quality time together that enhances their physical and emotional health. Physical activity reduces stress, elevates mood, and increases self-esteem, all of which contribute to a healthy marriage.

Another advantage of exercise is that it naturally improves mood. Dopamine and serotonin, which are released during exercise, are believed to boost happiness and lower anxiety. By committing to maintaining their physical and emotional well-being, couples create a positive cycle that strengthens their bond and deters hopelessness.

- ***Cultivate the Habit of Being Mindful and Engage in Spiritual Practices***

Incorporating spiritual practices and cultivating the act of being mindful into everyday life has been shown to have a grounding impact on many couples. Couples improve their mental and emotional awareness by meditating on the word of God together, or even just spending a few minutes each day in silence. Mindfulness exercises improve empathy, cultivate thankfulness, and lessen anxiety—all of which improves marriages and prevents disputes from becoming worse. A feeling of greater purpose is fostered by shared spiritual or mindful activities, as partners help one another achieve inner serenity and personal development.

These exercises encourage introspection, enabling couples to disentangle themselves from depressive or fixated emotions and enabling them to see their connection objectively.

- ***Performing Deeds of Service and Kindness Together***

Giving back to the community is a great way for couples to acquire perspective and deepen their relationship. Volunteering or doing deeds of kindness jointly serves as a reminder to both parties of the influence they have outside of their marriage. In order to avoid the self-centered concentration that may sometimes result in obsessive behavior in marriages, working together to assist others fosters empathy, compassion, and mutual respect.

Couples might find a constructive and healthy way to release their energy via community service. Couples who put others' needs first are able to see their own difficulties more clearly and often come to appreciate how lucky they are to have each other's support. Additionally, volunteering creates happy memories and shared experiences that deepen their marriage by bringing new levels of purpose and thankfulness.

- ***Develop an Attitude of Appreciation and Gratitude.***

As time passes, couples may find themselves taking each other for granted. Over time, couples may fail to recognize the little gestures of love and support they provide to one another, which may cause discontent and animosity. In order to maintain a happy and successful marriage, couples prevent emotions of hopelessness or undervaluation by developing an attitude of thankfulness.

Expressing gratitude to one another, whether via words, notes, or tiny gestures of kindness, should become a daily or weekly practice for couples. Mutual regard and emotional connection should be encouraged by consistently praising one other's excellent traits. By focusing on positive affirmations rather than always seeking confirmation, practicing gratitude also lowers the likelihood of obsessive attachment.

- ***Establish Customs and Practices***

Couples can depend on practices and traditions—small, significant routines—especially in trying times. Couples feel safe and connected by establishing touch points via simple routines like a weekly date night, morning coffee, or a nocturnal check-in. These customs might serve as reassuring reminders of a couple's connection and dedication to one another.

Establishing customs helps couples feel less hopeless by fostering a sense of continuity and a shared past. Additionally, practices give the relationship structure and give partners something to look forward to, which helps avoid the boredom that may sometimes result in emotions of reliance or alienation.

- ***If necessary, seek professional assistance***

Despite their best efforts, couples may sometimes find it difficult to overcome emotional obstacles. Seeking assistance from a relationship therapist, life coach, or a pastor, may be quite beneficial in these situations. Therapy provides a safe environment for couples to talk about their issues, develop good communication techniques, and see harmful behaviors that could be fueling their addiction or hopelessness.

Professional advice may be particularly helpful when couples are coping with particular issues like trauma, stress, or bereavement. In order to assist both spouses achieve balance and rebuild their marriage, a therapist may provide strategies for navigating challenging emotions. Asking for assistance is a proactive and constructive move that demonstrates a dedication to the well-being of your marriage.

You will agree with me that finding meaningful activities todo individually and separately is the key to staying active as a couple. Open communication, personal autonomy, shared interests, and community service all contribute to a healthy and satisfying relationship. Couples can maintain a healthy and fulfilling relationship and lower their risk of dejection or obsessive reliance by cultivating their unique and joint interests, establishing objectives, and practicing appreciation will allow their marriage to stand and thrive. By establishing a foundation of respect, understanding, and emotional stability, these behaviors enable both partners to flourish and take pleasure in a long-lasting, healthy marriage.

How Do I Keep Myself Focused on God and Productive Activities

Staying focused on God and engaging in constructive activities must go hand in hand in a marriage. Strong marriages are built on a solid connection with God, progress and satisfaction that comes from doing meaningful activities. It is the responsibility of Christian spouses to keep God at the center of their life and marriage and let Him direct their words, deeds, and goals. Couples may create a bond that embodies Christ's love, endures hardships, and benefits those around them by consciously concentrating on God and leading meaningful lives.

Christian couples can put God at the core of their relationship and continue to participate in fruitful activities that deepen their faith and connection by following these important guidelines I am about to discuss right now.

- ***Cultivate the Habit of Praying together as Couples***

One of the most effective ways to improve any Christian relationship, particularly in marriage, is through prayer. Couples that pray together bring God into their everyday choices and lives, gaining strength and togetherness from Him in the process. Refocusing on God and bringing our thoughts in line with His will can be achieved by scheduling time for prayer as a couple at the dawn and dusk of each day.

Morning prayers might center on praying for courage to face any obstacles that lie ahead, asking for help in making choices, and expressing thanks for the new day.

Evening prayers allow you a chance to think back on the day, give thanks to God for all that you have, and ask for forgiveness for any errors you may have made. Praying together strengthens a couple's spiritual and emotional bond by encouraging honest communication with God and one another.

- ***Study and Read the Bible Together Often***

One of the best ways for Christian couples to remain rooted in God's Word is to read the Bible together. The scripture offers guidance, support, and insight for leading a Christ-centered life as a couple and as individuals. Couples will better grasp God's plan, implement biblical principles in their relationship, and delve further into His teachings by scheduling time for Bible study.

To begin, couples might choose a book or chapter of the Bible to study together or choose devotionals that are appropriate for their present stage of life. Having conversations on the passage allows both parties to learn new things and hear viewpoints that they would not have otherwise thought about. Together, you memorize the Scriptures during Bible study, building a solid foundation of Scripture to rely on throughout both happy and difficult times.

- ***Participate in volunteer work or ministry together.***

Christian couples are expected to serve others and change the world in addition to fostering their personal relationship. As Christ lived a life of service, serving together in voluntary work or ministry mirrors his passion. Doing this helps us to be focused and helps us to overcome distractions in whatever way it may seem to raise its ugly heads against us. In addition to strengthening their relationship, couples fulfill God's call to love and serve others by volunteering in their local church or giving back to the society.

Couples may serve together in a variety of ways, including leading a Bible study group, serving at a food pantry, assisting at church functions, or going on mission trips. In addition to improving a couple's marriage, serving others gives them a sense of direction and serves as a reminder of their own benefits. Couples get closer to God and to one another as they cooperate to spread the love of Christ.

For instance, a couple may decide to attend a marital retreat or a series of Bible studies for couples if they want to develop their spirituality. A financial objective may include saving for a good cause or demonstrating stewardship by regularly tithing. When couples connect their objectives with God's ideas, they create a meaningful life together that demonstrates their devotion to Him.

- ***Worship and Fellowship Together as a Couple***

Christian couples can attain a strong spiritual foundation by regularly participating in worship and spending time with other Christians. Couples can participate in communal worship by going to church services, worship gatherings, or small groups together. This helps them feel more supported by other believers and deepens their faith in Christ Jesus.

- ***Practice showing grace and forgiveness Daily***

It takes constant grace and forgiveness to live out God's love, particularly in marriage. Although disagreements, miscommunications, and errors are unavoidable, God's love is shown when they are handled with compassion and forgiveness. Couples can preserve peace, togetherness and prevent the bitterness and animosity that can wreak havoc in their marriage by forgiving one another on a regular basis.

To let go of grudges and decide to love in spite of imperfections and errors are two aspects of forgiveness. In a marriage where both spouses feel appreciated and respected, showing grace to one another mirrors God's own kindness toward us. Couples who prioritize forgiveness and grace are better able to deal with difficulties without allowing resentment or disappointment to fester and instead concentrate on their own development. Remember, love covers multitude of sin; this is well captured in 1 Peter 4:8.

- ***Keep a Joint Gratitude Journal***

Gratitude is a means to maintain God at the heart of amarriage. Couples can maintain a joint gratitude journal inwhich they alternately list daily blessings for which theyare grateful to God for, doing this will keep them focusedand help them not to look at the distractions surrounding them. This practice serves to remind couples of God's love and faithfulness while refocusing their attention from grievances or disappointments to the positives in their life.

Couples might dedicate a certain amount of time each day or week to write down certain things for which they are thankful for, both separately and together. These might include little happy experiences as well as important prayers that are answered. Couples who frequently reflect on these benefits grow closer to one another and enhance their faith by acknowledging God's constant presence in their lives.

- ***Make Healthy Communication a Priority***

The foundation of every successful marriage is sound, God-centered communication. God's values of respect and love are upheld by couples who try to talk politely, listen intently, and settle disputes in a loving way. Couples must speak honestly about their emotions, ideas, and worries because God wants harmony and understanding.

Invoking God in prayer during talks, particularly challenging ones assists couples in approaching one another with compassion and humility. Christian couples can avoid misunderstandings, resolve conflicts amicably, and preserve their feeling of harmony and intimacy by placing a high value on polite communication. Additionally, this practice prevents partners from holding grudges, which may strain their bond and divert them from their spiritual journey.

- ### *Balance Work, Relaxation, and Leisure*

God commands us to have balanced lifestyles that include a career or business, relaxation, and leisure. Work and obligations are vital, but in order to maintain a strong and vibrant marriage, couples must also make time for relaxation and leisure. Whether it's via travel, hobbies, or just lounging around the house, spending time together to enjoy your marriage builds a balanced lifestyle that keeps burnout at bay and fortifies the bond between couples.

When God established the Sabbath, He set an example of rest, and it is crucial for couples to emulate Him by taking time off from work and obligations. Spending quality time relaxing together enables couples to rejuvenate, concentrate on God, and really appreciate one another's presence staying focused on God and engaging in productive activities. Recreation helps couples maintain a happy, balanced existence focused on God. Examples of this include spending time with family, taking part in common activities, and enjoying outdoor games and so on.

- ### *Support One Another's Spiritual Growth*

A Christ-centered marriage must include mutual support for one another's spiritual growth. By sharing personal spiritual discoveries, holding each other responsible for areas of spiritual development, and validating one other's faith, couples will actively support one another in their spiritual journey.

A spiritually encouraging atmosphere is created by routinely talking about spiritual objectives, difficulties, or revelations from the Bible. The other spouse may also provide support, prayers, and direction when one partner is having spiritual difficulties. Spiritual challenges may also be established by couples, including memorizing scriptures together or joining a Bible study group. Supporting one another's spiritual growth builds a marriage based on faith and shows Christ's love.

- ***Avoid Distractions and Set Boundaries.***

Distractions from social media and job demands are common in modern life, and they drive couples away from God and one another. Couples stay focused on the important things by establishing limits about technology, job schedules, and social obligations. Limiting screen time, for instance, particularly during meals or prayer time, enables couples to be totally focused on God and one other.

Establishing boundaries also entails putting one's marriage and spiritual obligations ahead of outside demands. By setting out time for Bible study, prayer, and quality time, couples can create a solid, distraction-free foundation for their marriage. Setting boundaries gives couples the clarity and concentration necessary to have a productive and God-centered life.

Any Christian couple hoping to build a strong, happy, and purposeful marriage must keep God at the core of their relationship. Christian's couples must keep focused on God and take part in constructive and productive activities that will improve their connection by actively practicing their spirituality, encouraging open communication, helping others, and leading balanced lifestyles. Couples can only develop together and deal with life's obstacles with grace and resiliency thanks to these practices, which provide a foundation of faith, love, and purpose. Christian couples can enjoy a marriage that reflects God's love and is a powerful message to others if they follow and focus on His guidance while engaging in productive activities.

Suggestions for Hobbies, Serving Others, and Activities to Stay Occupied

Being a Christian couple is a journey of faith, friendship, and growth that offers chances to deepen one's relationship with God as well as other human connections. Couples often struggle to maintain their engagement and fulfillment in the midst of hectic lifestyles, and discovering similar interests or hobbies may be a potent method to strengthen your bond, stay occupied while upholding

Christian principles. A rewarding opportunity to spend time together, foster their spiritual development, and give back to their community is to include hobbies, volunteer work, and meaningful activities.

For Christian couples, there's a need for couples to know that staying busy is a defense mechanism, which I will be discussing shortly. I will also share with you activities that serve as practical tools to keep couples busy defending their marriage from satanic manipulations. I will also unveil to you a wide range of ideas for fun time, volunteer opportunities, and activities keeping both parties occupied. These suggestions are intended to assist couples, whether they are celebrating decades together or are just getting married, develop as spiritual partners and enhance their lives by keeping them busy in meaningful, joyful ways.

However, before I share these suggestions that will enable couples from being distracted, I want to share with you the advantages of staying busy as couples.

Staying Busy Serves as a Protective Strategy

The mind is less vulnerable to harmful impulses when it is intentionally active. Choosing activities that enhance one's well-being, happiness, or personal development is a better way to stay occupied than just cramming one's schedule with pointless things. Because of this deliberate activity, the mind is kept engaged, focused, and aware, which makes it difficult for harmful ideas to establish themselves. The more active and healthier the mind, the more it can guard against negative effects. Think of the mind as a mental immune system.

Taking part in positive activities also fosters a feeling of contentment, purpose, and success. Since they increase resilience, confidence, and self-worth, these positive feelings act as a barrier against the falsehoods of the adversary. For example, picking up a new activity or talent pushes the mind and gives one a feeling of accomplishment. People are reminded of their value and worth in a society through social events, which also serve to build connections and support.

It Impacts Purposeful Participation

Keeping a busy schedule requires more than simply distraction; it requires deliberate engagement. When couples engage in activities that align with their values, goals, and interests, their lives and marriage take a new turn. Engaging in purposeful activities fosters a sense of meaning, which is a potent remedy for depressing or empty emotions. According to psychological research, having a sense of purpose is crucial for mental health, and those who have a stronger sense of purpose are less likely to experience anxiety, depression, or other mental health conditions.

Purposeful activity also increases consciousness, which strengthens couples' defenses against unfavorable thoughts. We set aside concerns about the past or the future when we are totally engaged in what we are doing, whether it is writing, painting, cooking, or working out. People who practice mindfulness are able to identify unpleasant ideas without being overwhelmed by them. For example, if someone has a moment of self-doubt, they may identify it and, by engaging in a task mindfully, refocus their attention so that the doubt doesn't turn into hopelessness. This is particularly crucial because it prevents negative ideas from intensifying and taking precedence over constructive or good ideas.

It brings out the Value of Goal-Setting

Setting and achieving goals gives you the direction, structure, and drive you need to keep occupied in a meaningful manner. It's simple to feel that time is being squandered or that efforts are pointless when there are no objectives. People, who make reasonable, attainable objectives, no matter how large or little, establish benchmarks that keep them motivated and engaged. Personal and professional goals are both acceptable as long as they are clear and significant. Setting objectives gives couples a feeling of purpose for every work they embark on, this enables them to celebrate successes, and tracks their progress.

A person who is lonely, for instance, can decide to join a group or community club in order to meet others. Small, quantifiable actions, such as volunteering or going to meetings, helps couples to gradually create a network of social support that helps to lessen feelings of loneliness. In order to feel better about them and make progress, someone who is struggling with self-doubt could decide to acquire a new talent or become better at an existing hobby. Setting goals helps couples close the gap between where they are and where they want to be by directing them toward activities that improve their general wellbeing.

Helps to Keep Relationships and Community as Anchors

Since humans are social animals by nature, having deep relationships with other people is crucial for our mental health. Loneliness and isolation create an environment that is conducive to the spread of falsehoods by the enemy. In the absence of social reinforcement, negative self-perceptions intensify making people feel unwanted or undeserving. Couples have a sense of belonging that combats these negative emotions by continuing to be involved in a community, whether it be via friends, family, or organizations based on common interests.

Participating in their community gives them access to a support system that provides companionship, support, and constructive criticism. One might feel more grounded and less likely to give in to emotions of dread or despair when they know that there are trustworthy and kind individuals in the world. In addition to keeping the body and mind busy, group-based activities like volunteer work, sports, and courses also help people feel connected, which makes it easier to resist negative influences.

Having opened your eyes to the advantages that staying busy can do for you as couples, I will like to get down to the business of discussing probable suggestions couples can engage to stay occupied.

Spiritual Hobbies: Growing Faith Together

Bible Study and Prayer Time for Christian Couples

As earlier discussed in the previous chapters, Bible study and prayer time is very vital for Christian couples. It provides them a chance to deepen their and provides spiritual support to one another. This can entail following a particular devotional plan, reading passages aloud, or sharing interpretations. Couples strengthen their spiritual ties by praying for one another, sharing their worries, giving thanks to God during a dedicated prayer time.

Learning Scripture by Heart

Scripture memorization is a potent method for couples looking for an enjoyable and fulfilling task to help them absorb God's word. Couples can choose important verses that speak to them and then alternate reciting them, playing memory games, or discussing how these verses affect their life and marriage.

Christian Book Club for Two

Examining Christian literatures can provide insights to your marriage and faith, as well as ignite thought-provoking conversations amongst couples. Every week, couples can schedule time to study a chapter from a Christian book and then meet together to talk about what they learnt. Whether it's a book about marriage, or personal development, this shared experience can be enlightening and stimulating.

Engaging in Sessions of Worship

Couples might think about scheduling worship music sessions if one or both of them are musically inclined. Coming together to sing or play an instrument enhances their worship to God and a euphoria of joy is created in their marriage. A casual interest in music can be transformed into a spiritually uplifting time by making a worship playlist, singing together, or even writing songs together.

Serving Others: Spreading Love throughout the Neighborhood

Church Volunteering

One of the best ways for couples to serve together is to volunteer in church. Participating in hospitality ministries, assisting with Sunday school, planning events, or joining the worship team are all ways to serve the church and community. Couples can get involved in the church community by determining where their special talents or interests fit in the best.

Joining Campaigns for Outreach

Another way couples can stay occupied is by joining campaigns for outreaches. Christian couples might think about getting involved in community service projects like feeding the homeless, visiting the elderly or interacting with patients in rehab facilities. Outreach enables couples to cultivate empathy, acquire a more comprehensive understanding of God's action in the world, marriage and discover a purpose that extends beyond them.

Engaging in Missionary Trips

Mission trips have the potential to change the lives of people who are willing to put in the effort. Mission trips, whether domestic or foreign, provide couples the chance to collaborate in trying situations while helping others in need. Together, they may strengthen their relationship as they go out on their journey by praying, collecting money, and studying the cultural way of life, thereby avoiding distraction in whatever form it may take.

Organizing Fellowship Dinners or Bible studies

Couples who like entertaining people may invite friends or neighbors over for fellowship meals or Bible studies in their home. A warm environment is created via hosting people to develop in God's word, share their faith, and enjoy company. For Christian couples who like hospitality, cooking, praying at events, and fostering conversation may be fulfilling experiences.

Growth and Fun Activities: Strengthens Your Bond

A prayer journal or a couple's journal

Couples may document their shared experiences, prayer requests, answered prayers, and special events by keeping a joint diary. They can also consider how God has been at work in their marriage or send encouraging words to one another. This practice develops into a lovely memento that chronicles their shared spiritual journey.

Attending Workshops or Courses

Learning something new together is also one of the activities that can ensure couples stay occupied. It strengthens a Christian couple's relationship and encourages teamwork. This may include going to Bible study classes, marital enrichment seminars, or even lessons on practical skills (such cooking, gardening, or photography) that let them develop as a couple. Nowadays numerous Christian groups and churches have embraced the ideas of providing retreats that blend education with relaxation and rejuvenation for a more immersive experience.

Engaging in Fitness and Wellness Activities

Living a happy life and serving others can only be achieved when couples maintain good health. Jogging, hiking, or going to the gym together are examples of physical activities that couples might engage in. In order to take care of their bodies and souls, individuals might also attempt relaxing and health-promoting hobbies like taking nature walks. This becomes much more meaningful if you set fitness objectives or prepare for a charity race.

Engage in Creative Hobbies

Couples can decide to take up hobbies like painting, crafts, writing, or photography if one or both of them are creatively inclined. Couples may even attempt creating presents for friends and family as well as engaging in self-expression and relaxation via these hobbies. Making homemade Christmas cards or writing customized comments, for example, may give the gift-giving and holiday seasons a more significant touch.

Spending Quality Time and Engaging in Recreational Activities: Revitalizing your Marriage

A Twist on Date Nights

Date evenings take on new significance when faith is included. During a "Faith Date Night," couples may go to a worship concert, see a Christian film, or travel to a beautiful place to pray and discuss their aspirations. Frequent date evenings are crucial for reestablishing contact and enhancing the enjoyment of the marriage shunning distractions. You can engage in ABC dinner date. Pick a letter from the alphabets, and pick a date around that letter. Also pick a day in the week just for a date.

Exploring Nature Together

For couples who are outdoor enthusiasts, spending time in nature is a revitalizing way to reestablish relationships with God and one another. In hiking, camping, or just strolling in a nearby park, couples discover tranquility, appreciate God's creation, and contemplate the beauty of nature. Some couples may even study scripture or pray outside on a regular basis.

Baking and Cooking Together

Baking or cooking may be a fun and useful time to stay occupied for couples. Bonding over common duties can be achieved by trying out new recipes, cooking meals together, or even creating delights to share with friends or neighbors. Learning about various cultures may also be enjoyable when you try foods from other cultures.

Engaging in Puzzles or Games

Solving puzzles and playing card and board games can be a pleasant and enjoyable way to relax for couples who like intellectual challenges and friendly rivalry. There are many games with Christian themes, or they might play more generic games that encourage cooperation and communication.

Goal-setting and Personal Growth

Establishing Spiritual and Individual Goals

Couples should cultivate the habit of coming together to talk about their shared and personal goals at the start of the year or whenever they feel the need. This may include interpersonal objectives (like enhancing communication or spending more time together), financial or professional ambitions, and spiritual goals (like developing in prayer or starting a new ministry). Regularly reviewing these goals help to keep couples on the same page and encourage one another towards achieving the set goals.

Supporting Each Other's Personal Interests

It is crucial for couples to encourage one another's own interests. Even while it's crucial to have activities together, each partner may have interests they like on their own which keeps them occupied. Supporting one another in their interests, whether they are reading, gardening, athletics, or the arts, demonstrates respect for one another and allows each person to develop as a unique individual.

Engage in Consistent Thanksgiving and Reflection

For Christian couples, making time for introspection and gratitude should become a habit. Every week or every month, couples should embrace the habit of discussing their blessings and how they see God's influence in their life and marriage. They should also think back on the growth they have experienced in their marriage. doing this would enable them to work hand in hand to stand for their marriage thereby avoiding distractions and focusing on God. Practicing the act of gratitude helps couples to stay optimistic about life and keeps them focused on God's blessings.

Hobbies, volunteer work, and meaningful activities are more than simply ways for Christian couples to stay occupied; they are a means of strengthening their bond and fostering their faith. Whether they are expanding their understanding of God's word, helping others in need, or just spending time together, these pursuits provide the groundwork for a rewarding and purpose-driven marriage. In the end, Christian couples who devote time to these common interests experience significant growth in their marriage and in their connection with God. Together, they are creating a life that provides them joy, purpose, and peace while also honoring God as they make time for their faith, service, and personal pleasure a priority.

A dedication to self-care and self-awareness is necessary for the discipline of staying occupied in order to stop the adversary's falsehoods. It is more than just packing the day full of activities; it involves choosing to actively pursue activities that foster development, resiliency, and wellbeing. Couples may reduce their vulnerability to harmful ideas or influences by directing or redirecting their time and energy toward meaningful activities that will provide a calm and productive mental environment.

Staying occupied with purpose is essentially a way to develop resilience, mental toughness, constructive habits, and self-defense. It calls for an active outlook on life, a will to improve personally, and a refusal to allow inactivity or stagnation to make room for pessimism. By means of intentional involvement, goal-setting, mindfulness, and community connection, couples can successfully protect themselves from the falsehoods of the adversary and regain mastery over their thoughts and feelings. It prevents negativity and promotes a more balanced and purposeful marriage for couples.

Chapter 8

Place Premium On God'S Word In Fighting For Your Marriage

Marriage is an incredible journey, full of joy, companionship, and personal growth, but it's no secret that it can also be challenging. When difficulties arise, where do you turn for guidance and strength? For Christians, the answer lies in God's Word. The Bible offers wisdom and comfort that can transform how we navigate marriage, giving us tools to resolve conflicts, heal wounds, and build intimacy. Let's dive into why God's Word is so central to marriage and how it can be your lifeline as you fight for the health and happiness of your relationship.

Why God's Word is Central to Marriage

To truly understand why God's Word is so important in marriage, it helps to look back at how marriage began. Marriage was God's idea—He created it and designed it to be a sacred covenant between two people. In Genesis, we see how God created Eve for Adam as a companion, a helper, and someone with whom he could do life with. From the start, God's vision for marriage was one of partnership, unity, and mutual love.

Scripture gives us a blueprint for how marriage should work. It's not just about finding happiness or companionship; it's about a deep, spiritual commitment to one another. Ephesians 5:25 calls husbands to love their wives "just as Christ loved the church and gave himself up for her." That's an incredibly powerful directive, setting a standard for selfless love, patience, and sacrifice. Similarly, wives are encouraged to respect and support their husbands in ways that foster mutual trust and appreciation. By following these principles, couples can build relationships that mirror the love and respect that God intended.

When a couple roots their marriage in God's Word, they are essentially choosing to build their foundation on something eternal and unchanging. In times of hardship, that foundation becomes a source of strength, offering wisdom and perspective beyond what either partner could muster alone. So many couples try to "do marriage" on their own terms, drawing from cultural ideas or personal desires that often fall short. But when we lean into the wisdom of Scripture, we tap into guidance that has stood the test of time.

Using Scripture as a Guide for Conflict Resolution

Let's face it: every marriage encounter conflict. Whether it's a misunderstanding, a hurtful comment, or even a betrayal of trust, conflicts in marriage are inevitable. But how we handle those conflicts can make all the difference between a marriage that grows stronger and one that becomes strained and disconnected. This is where God's Word can be a powerful tool. All marriages has its ups and downs; there's no perfect marriage.

The Bible is filled with practical advice for handling conflict. In James 1:19, we're reminded to be "quick to listen, slow to speak, and slow to become angry." This simple principle can transform arguments, helping each partner approach conflicts with patience and a desire to understand the other's perspective. Proverbs 15:1 teaches that "a gentle answer turns away wrath, but a harsh word stirs up anger." Imagine if both spouses committed to responding gently, even when emotions were running high. This doesn't mean avoiding hard conversations or suppressing emotions, but choosing words and actions that lead to understanding rather than escalation. When talking with your partner, always ask yourself; "Does my conversation represent these 3Ps – Humility, Honesty and Honorable?"

Forgiveness is another cornerstone of resolving conflict, and the Bible has so much to say about it. In Colossians 3:13, we are told to "bear with each other and forgive one another if any of you has a grievance against someone. Forgive as the Lord forgave you." Forgiveness doesn't mean ignoring hurt or pretending something didn't happen. Rather, it's about choosing to release resentment and let go of grudges, just as God continually forgives us. This practice can be incredibly freeing in marriage, allowing couples to move past mistakes and start fresh rather than letting issues pile up and cause bitterness.

Healing Wounds with the Help of God's Word

Wounds in marriage come in many forms—misunderstandings, broken promises, unmet expectations, and more. While some hurts may be small and easily forgiven, others can cut deep, making it hard to rebuild trust and closeness. God's Word offers comfort, hope, and a path to healing for those wounds, reminding us that healing is possible when we rely on Him.

Psalm 147:3 tells us, "He heals the brokenhearted and binds up their wounds." This verse shows us that God cares deeply about our pain and is willing to help us heal. When a spouse hurts us, it's natural to want to shut down, protect ourselves, or even seek revenge. But God's way is different—He calls us to turn to Him with our pain, trusting that He can mend our hearts and help us forgive. By bringing our wounds to God, we can find the strength to move forward and let love and forgiveness transform our marriage.

Scripture also encourages us to examine ourselves and take responsibility for our actions. In Matthew 7:3-5, Jesus teaches about looking at the "plank" in our own eye before focusing on the "speck" in someone else's. In marriage, this means being willing to acknowledge our own shortcomings and work on them rather than always pointing fingers. This honest self-evaluation can create an atmosphere of humility and grace, helping both partners feel safe enough to be vulnerable and authentic.

Building Intimacy Through God's Word

Intimacy in marriage is more than just physical closeness; it's about emotional and spiritual connection. God's Word plays a vital role in building and sustaining this kind of intimacy, as it encourages couples to nurture their spiritual bond. When couples pray together, study the Bible together, and have open communication, they strengthen the bond between them and God.

Ecclesiastes 4:12 speaks of a "cord of three strands," symbolizing a marriage that includes God at the center. When both partners are committed to walking with God, their relationship naturally deepens as they share a common purpose and direction. Praying together, for instance, is a powerful act of intimacy. It opens the door to understanding each other's deepest hopes, fears, and dreams while inviting God's guidance and peace into the relationship.

Additionally, studying Scripture together can spark meaningful conversations that draw you closer. Talking about how God's Word applies to your lives as individuals and as a couple helps you grow spiritually and build a sense of unity. By seeking God's wisdom together, you align your goals, values, and priorities, making it easier to support each other and work toward shared dreams.

The Spiritual Significance of Applying God's Word in Marriage

Applying God's Word in marriage goes beyond conflict resolution, healing, or intimacy; it invites a spiritual transformation that can profoundly impact both partners and their family. When you live out biblical principles in marriage, you create a home filled with love, peace, and respect. This atmosphere not only strengthens your bond but also becomes a testimony to others of God's grace and power.

Moreover, as you practice love, patience, forgiveness, and humility—qualities God's Word emphasizes—you grow as individuals. Marriage becomes a journey of personal and spiritual development, where each partner is refined and strengthened. By seeking God's guidance, you develop resilience, perseverance, and faith, knowing that God is working in and through your marriage.

Specific Scriptures for Issues in Marriage

When it comes to marriage, we know it's not always a walk in the park. Relationships go through ups and downs, and it can be challenging to know how to navigate the tough spots. Thankfully, the Bible offers plenty of wisdom for just about any marital struggle you can think of. Whether it's communication, forgiveness, intimacy, or conflict, the Word has something powerful to say about it. Let's dive into some key scriptures that can guide you through these common struggles.

1. Communication Issues

Good communication is essential for any relationship, but especially in marriage. When words hurt instead of heal, it can be tough to connect. That's why the Bible offers clear guidance on how to speak to each other in a way that builds up. Proverbs 15:1 says a gentle answer turns away wrath, but a harsh word stirs up anger." When things get heated, remember this verse. A soft, kind response can de-escalate a tense situation, while harsh words only add fuel to the fire. Try to stay calm, choose your words wisely, and focus on speaking with grace.

Also consider this verse; Ephesians 4:29 - "Do not let any unwholesome talk come out of your mouths, but only what is helpful for building others up according to their needs, that it may benefit those who listen." This verse is a reminder to speak with purpose. Every word you say should be constructive, aimed at building up your spouse rather than tearing them down.

2. Forgiveness

Every marriage will face moments where one partner hurts the other—intentionally or unintentionally. What matters most is how you handle those wounds. Forgiveness is key. Colossians 3:13 encourages us to bear with each other and forgive one another just as the Lord forgave us. This is a strong reminder that forgiveness isn't optional. Just as God has forgiven us, we are called to forgive each other. It may be hard, but it's essential for healing and moving forward. Also, in Matthew 18:21-22, Jesus calls us to forgive as often as needed—no matter how many times someone offends us. It's about letting go of bitterness and giving grace freely, just as we've received it.

3. Intimacy

Intimacy goes beyond the physical. It's about being emotionally, mentally, and spiritually connected. When intimacy starts to fade in marriage, it's important to lean into God's plan for oneness because God's designed sexual intimacy to strengthen the bond between a husband and wife. 1 Corinthians 7:3-4 says the husband should fulfill his marital duty to his wife, and likewise the wife to her husband because the wife's body does not belong to her alone but also to her husband. In the same way, the husband's body does not belong to him alone but also to his wife. This scripture emphasizes the mutual responsibility partners have toward each other. Intimacy is a two-way street, and both spouses should prioritize each other's needs, emotionally and physically. Songs of Solomon 4:9-10 paints a beautiful picture of romantic love and passion. It reminds us that marital intimacy can be a beautiful expression of love and devotion.

4. Conflict Resolution

Disagreements are inevitable, but how we handle them can make or break a relationship. The Bible teaches us how to handle conflict in a way that preserves the marriage. James 1:19-20, encourages us to be quick to listen, slow to speak and slow to become angry, because human anger does not produce the righteousness that God desires. This verse is perfect for when tempers flare. Instead of jumping into a heated argument, take a step back. Listen carefully, speak slowly, and try to approach the situation with a calm and patient heart. In times of conflict, strive to be a peacemaker. Sometimes, this means letting go of your own pride for the sake of unity and harmony in your marriage.

5. Unity

A strong marriage is built on unity—on the deep understanding that you and your spouse are in this together, through thick and thin. Genesis 2:24 explains that a man leaves his father and mother and clings to his wife, and they become one flesh. Which shows us that marriage is meant to create unity. Two people become one, both in heart and in purpose. It's a bond that should not be broken. In Ephesians 5:31-32, Paul highlights the deep, spiritual significance of marriage. Just as Christ and the church are united, so too should husband and wife be united. It's about commitment and a shared purpose. This means that couples should speak with one voice on all issues.

6. Sacrifice

Sacrificial love is at the core of a healthy marriage. It's not always easy, but putting your spouse's needs above your own is what creates a lasting and fulfilling bond. Apostle Paul in Ephesians 5:25 says, husbands to love their wives, just as Christ loved the church and gave himself up for her. This is a call for husbands to love sacrificially, just as

Christ sacrificed everything for the church. It's about putting your spouse's needs first, even when it's tough. Sacrificial love isn't just for husbands; it's for both spouses. Marriage calls both partners to put each other first, even when it requires self-sacrifice. John 15:13.

Pray God's Word to Reality in Your Marriage

Praying God's Word into your marriage is one of the most powerful things you can do to strengthen your relationship and invite God's transforming presence into your lives. When we pray Scripture, we're not only connecting with God, but we're also standing on the promises He's given us in His Word. Let's explore what it means to pray Scripture over your marriage, why it's so effective, and some practical steps for getting started.

The Power of Praying Scripture

The Bible tells us that "the word of God is alive and active" (Hebrews 4:12). God's Word isn't just words on a page; it's living and powerful, able to bring change, healing, and restoration. When you pray Scripture over your marriage, you're aligning your heart and desires with God's will for your relationship. It's a way of saying, "Lord, I believe in Your promises, and I trust that You're at work in our marriage."

Praying Scripture also allows you to speak God's truth into your situation. Instead of relying on your own words, you're praying words that are already backed by God's authority and power. It's like planting seeds of God's promises in the soil of your marriage, trusting that in time, they'll grow into reality.

Examples of Prayers for Specific Marital Issues

To make praying Scripture easier, here are some specific prayers for common issues couples face. These prayers are drawn from the Bible, helping you connect God's Word directly to your relationship.

1. For Unity and Love

Unity and love are the foundation of a strong marriage. Ask God to fill you and your spouse with a love that mirrors His. "Lord, help us to love each other as You have loved us. Make us one in spirit and purpose, bringing us closer together in every way. May our love be patient, kind, and sacrificial, just as You have shown us in Your love" (based on Ephesians 5:25).

2. For Communication

Communication is vital for a healthy relationship, and sometimes, we need God's help to speak kindly and listen well. "Father, teach us to listen to each other with open hearts and to speak with kindness and understanding. Let our words be seasoned with grace and wisdom, building each other up instead of tearing down. Help us to communicate in ways that reflect Your love and peace" (based on Proverbs 15:1, James 1:19).

3. For Forgiveness

Forgiveness is essential in any relationship. When you pray for God's help to forgive, you're inviting Him to heal past hurts and prevent bitterness from taking root. "Lord, help us to forgive each other just as You have forgiven us. Let no bitterness or resentment take root in our hearts. Give us the grace to let go of past offenses and extend mercy and kindness to one another every day" (based on Colossians 3:13, Ephesians 4:32).

4. For Peace in Conflict

Conflict is inevitable, but God's Word can guide us in handling it with grace and peace. "God, guide us in resolving conflicts peacefully, with humility and understanding. Help us not to let the sun go down on our anger but to seek reconciliation quickly and wholeheartedly. Fill our home with Your peace" (based on Ephesians 4:26).

Praying Together as a Couple

One of the most powerful ways to strengthen your marriage is to pray together as a couple. Praying together not only invites God's presence but also builds intimacy, trust, and emotional connection. When you and your spouse come together in prayer, you're showing each other that you're willing to seek God's will for your relationship.

Here are a few simple steps to make praying together feel natural and meaningful:

1. Start Small: Begin with short, focused prayers. You could start by praying one of the Scriptures above, taking turns each day.

2. Be Honest: Share what's on your heart with God and each other. It doesn't have to be perfect; it just needs to be real.

3. Pray for Each Other's Needs: Take turns praying for one another's personal needs as well as for your marriage. It shows love and support for each other.

4. Thank God Together: Gratitude is a powerful bond. Spend time thanking God for each other, for your blessings, and even for the challenges that help you grow together.

As you make a habit of praying together, you'll find that it builds a deep, spiritual connection that helps you face both joys and struggles as a team.

Faith and Action

Prayer is powerful, but it's only part of the equation. Faith requires action. James 2:17 reminds us that "faith without works is dead." While praying God's Word over your marriage, it's equally important to live out those prayers by actively working on your relationship.

Here are a few ways to put your prayers into action:

1. **For Unity and Love**: If you're praying for unity, look for ways to spend quality time together. Be intentional about shared activities, setting aside distractions, and truly connecting.

2. **For Communication**: If you're asking God to help you communicate better, practice listening with an open mind and speaking with kindness, even when it's difficult.

3. **For Forgiveness:** If you're praying for forgiveness, actively release past grievances. When old memories or hurts come up, remind yourself to forgive, as you've prayed.

4. **For Peace in Conflict:** If you're praying for peace, commit to walking away from arguments when they get heated. Take a moment to breathe, pray, and then come back to the conversation with a calm spirit.

Remember that prayer is an invitation for God to work in you and through you. While you're trusting Him to bring change, you're also responsible for doing your part. Faith and action go hand-in-hand in making your prayers a reality.

Bringing It All Together

Praying Scripture into your marriage isn't just a habit; it's a lifestyle of continually surrendering your relationship to God. When you pray with faith, speak God's promises, and take action, you're inviting Him to create a marriage that reflects His love, unity, forgiveness, and peace.

Marriage is a journey, with each step taken together and with God leading the way. So, start today, bringing God's Word to life in your marriage, and trust that He'll be faithful to guide, heal, and strengthen your relationship in ways you never thought possible.

Chapter 9

Stay The Course – Trusting God'S Plan

Are you perhaps losing your mind or hope due to a departed spouse? Keep standing! The lord is about to do a remarkable thing in your marriage. All you need do is to trust God.

Life might seem like a long journey with many unanticipated turns, steep hills to climb, and invisible obstacles. Christian couples may find out that these detours put their faith and teamwork to test. Even when the way is uncertain, maintaining a strong faith and dedication in your marriage is necessary to remain on course and believe in God's plan through every season, whether it be joyful or challenging.

Relying on God's time and wisdom, letting go of control, and accepting that He sees the wider picture are all parts of trusting His plan. For couples, it also involves supporting, depending on, and staying together through faith. In this chapter, I will be unraveling how Christian couples can strengthen their bond staying on course in their devotion to God and one another by trusting God's plan. And if your husband or wife has worked away, the following principles also apply.

Develop an Attitude of Prayer. Staying in touch with God's will requires prayer. The Bible encourages us to "cast all your anxiety on Him because He cares for you" (1 Peter 5:7), despite the fact that it's normal for couples to desire to resolve issues on their own when they encounter difficulties or uncertainties. Couples must trust God to handle their hopes, concerns, and choices by making prayer a regular part of their lives, trusting that He is in charge. Additionally, praying together fosters solidarity and creates space for couples to be vulnerable with each other. Couples strengthen their relationship with God and each other by using prayer to express their thankfulness as well as their worries. They find direction, serenity and comfort in knowing that they are following God's plan if they set aside time every day or every week to pray over their marriage, family, and future.

Pay attention to God's promises rather than the current situation. Examining God's promises in the scriptures provides clarity and hope when you're feeling uncertain. The situations we face in life are fleeting, but God's word endures forever, and His promises provide us with a solid foundation that empowers us to put our trust in Him. We are reminded that God has a purpose for every circumstance in the scriptures: Jeremiah 29:11, where He affirms,

"For I know the plans I have for you...plans to give you hope and a future."

Couples who study scripture together and remind one another of God's faithfulness find strength during trying times. Couples are encouraged to endure and have confidence that God is actively working for their welfare, even when they are unable to see it, by studying stories of faith and perseverance, such as those of Paul, Joseph, Abraham and so on.

In Times of Uncertainty, Choose Faith over Fear. Choosing faith over fear is sometimes easier said than done, particularly in situations that may appear hopeless or overwhelming. Fear may cause impatience and the desire to take charge, but faith necessitates a different strategy: letting go and letting God take the lead while you follow. By reinterpreting difficult situations as chances to further their spiritual growth and increase their dependence on God, couples can support one another by relying on God.

Listing some particular anxieties or worries and bringing them before God collectively will be helpful in times of uncertainty. The first step to overcoming fear is admitting it. Couples find solace in scriptures, in the book of Isaiah 41:10,

"Do not be dismayed, for I am your God; do not fear, for I am with you."

This serves as a reminder and an anchor to the couples of God's power and presence.

Develop a Closer Spiritual Bond. Marriage is a partnership, both in our daily life and in one's Christian faith. As a couple, staying the course means sticking by one another and drawing strength from one another. Open communication, common objectives, and mutual encouragement in faith should all be used to actively foster your marriage.

Studying the Bible together, going to church, or simply scheduling time to talk about what God is teaching each couple separately may help to develop a closer spiritual connection. Couples may also keep a joint or individual journal in which they record scriptural insights, prayers answered, and reflect on God's faithfulness. This practice keeps their hearts close and enables them to see God's hand at work in one another's lives.

Embrace God's Timing and Patience. It may seem difficult to wait for God's time, particularly in this day and age where instant gratification has become a norm. It's crucial for Christian couples to keep in mind that God's timetable does not always coincide with their own. by learning to wait patiently and with grace, believing that God is working things out for His ultimate purpose to be fulfilled in our marriage brings peace. Remember, God is not a genie in a bottle.

Couples might utilize the waiting period to be ready both practically and spiritually. This might include making an investment in one's own development, picking up new skills, or just strengthening one another's resilience. Couples should embrace the journey and let go of the need to be in a haste or control by keeping in mind that God "works all things together for those who love Him" (Romans 8:28).

Trust the Christian Community. The obstacles that arise from trusting in God's plan may sometimes seem insurmountable. In times like these, having a Christian community around oneself offers support, guidance, insight, and motivation. Couples may be on the lookout for others who share their beliefs, join small groups, get advice from mentors, or just become friends with other couples who are also Christian couples.

During challenging times, this community provides support and perspectives that will enhance couples' faith in God. Couples are reminded that they are not alone when they are around a strong Christian community, whether it is via group prayer, guidance from those who have had similar difficulties, or just the consolation of companionship. This strengthens their faith and their heart that they are in the midst of the right people thereby, they can be at ease.

Work Together to Turn Your Attention Outward. When obstacles seem insurmountable, it's easy to become inwardly focused and concentrate on one's own shortcomings. Nonetheless, making the decision to help others may change one's views and rekindle one's faith. Couples are reminded of God's love and the benefits they still have in spite of their present difficulties when they invest in helping others.

Serving one another might take the form of aiding a friend in need, volunteering at the church, or taking part in community service. Serving others not only strengthens a couple's bond but also helps them fulfill God's mandate to love others. They could experience a revitalized feeling of purpose, pleasure, and thankfulness as they turn their attention outward.

Keep in Mind Previous Victories as a Reminder of God's Dependability. Thinking back on previous victories reassures you that you can always depend on God to be faithful once more when doubts start to sneak in. Recalling instances when God answered their prayers, provided for them in unexpected ways, or helped them get through challenging times serves as a reminder to couples that they are not alone in life.

In order to document important times in their marriage or life journey when they saw God's hand at work, couples may decide to make a "faith timeline" together. This can be periods of healing and reconciliation, job opportunities, or even prayers being answered. Their hope that God will continue to guide them is strengthened by recalling His previous faithfulness and dependability.

Keep Your Identity Rooted in Christ. When things don't go as planned, it's easy for couples to feel under pressure or inadequate in a society that often emphasizes accomplishment, prestige, or material success. By keeping their identity rooted in Christ, couples remain rooted in the knowledge that God values them for who they are rather than what they achieve.

In the midst of setbacks or unforeseen circumstances, spouses supporting one another serves as a way of reminding each other that they are the apple of God's eye.

By concentrating on the timeless reality of God's love and grace, praying for one another, confirming each other's worth, and assisting one another, couples will see beyond the fleeting difficulties.

Appreciate God's Handiwork in the Little Things. Celebrating little triumphs, appreciating daily blessings, and peaceful moments of happiness are often part of staying the course. During difficult times, these little reminders boost our faith and inspire hope. Couples should continue to be grateful and in awe as they discover how God works every day in their lives.

It is possible for couples to develop the habit of routinely sharing little blessings which aren't little in God's eye, such as a prayer answered, a peaceful atmosphere or an unexpected act of kindness. By commemorating these, couples strengthen their conviction that God is leading them at every turn and that He is at work in everything, no matter how great or little.

It takes a journey of faith, endurance, and patience to trust God's plan. This journey is one that draws Christian couples closer to God and to one another, particularly when they decide to put their trust in His wisdom rather than their own. Couples are capable of overcoming obstacles in life with grace if they remain firmly anchored in prayer, concentrate on God's promises in the scriptures, and choose faith over fear.

Couples can believe that God's hand is at work at all times if they adopt a heart of service, patience, and thankfulness. They will discover as they travel the twisting roads of marriage together that it is one of the most rewarding routes, full of love, faith, and tenacity.

Maintaining Faith, Peace, and Hope While Waiting for God's Restoration

Waiting for God to restore can be one of the most tiring times in a believer's life. Even in the face of uncertainty, it calls for patience, unwavering hope, and steadfast faith. However, God's Word provides insight and inspiration for those who are in waiting seasons. Knowing that God is working for our ultimate good allows us to keep faith, peace, and hope by getting closer to Him and believing in His promises.

Here, I will critically examine biblical teachings and useful strategies for fostering these attributes while you wait on God to restore your life and marriage.

1. **Faith: *Trusting the Integrity and Promises of God***

Trusting God as who He claims to be, particularly in situations that are uncertain, is often necessary to keep one's faith while waiting.

Faith calls us to rely less on our knowledge of the circumstances and focus more on God's love, goodness and wisdom. Having faith in God's plan according to scriptures in Proverbs 3:5-6: *"Trust in the Lord with all your heart and lean not to your understanding, submit to Him in all your ways and He will direct your path"*. This verse of the scriptures serves as a potent reminder that God's ways are higher than ours and that He is leading us towards a purpose even when we are unable to see the result. We acknowledge that He has a plan even when it is not visible to us, when we put our trust in Him.

Make sure you keep in mind God's Faithfulness. Our faith and trust in God is strengthened when we reminisce on instances in the past where God proved Himself faithful. The scriptures remind us to *"meditate on all His works and "remember the deeds of the Lord"* in Psalms 77:11-12. Thinking back on God's previous faithfulness towards us helps as a reminder that He has and will continue to see us through difficult times.

Have faith in the Face of Adversity. Sounds hard right? Trials that test and sharpen us are common while we wait for restoration. Scriptures in James 1:2–4 also confirms it

"Consider it pure joy...whenever you bear trials of many kinds, for you know that the testing of your faith produces perseverance". As we wait for God's promises to come to pass, adversity helps us learn to rely on Him and wait for His promises to come to fulfillment in our lives and marriage.

Daily bible study and prayer is also very key in trusting God. Spending time with God as couples on a daily basis helps you to stay focused on His promises which in turn strengthens your trust.

Ensure you are in touch with other believers. Sharing your challenges to your mentors or friends who are Christians helps couples to stay accountable, encouraged and guide their journey of faith.

2. *Peace: Finding Serenity in the Presence of God*

Peace might seem elusive, particularly during uncertain times or when restoration appears far off. But the Bible affirms that peace exists in God's presence and is independent of other factors.

The Peace of Jesus Christ. Jesus assured His disciples that there would be peace surpasses comprehension of this world:

"Peace, I leave with you; my peace I give you. I do not give to you as the world gives. Do not let your heart be troubled and do not be afraid" (John 14:27). Knowing that God is in charge and with us in every circumstance is the foundation of this peace I am talking about.

Casting your fears on God. The scriptures gave us an assurance when we're faced with fears *"Do not be anxious about anything, but in every situation, by prayer and petition, with thanksgiving, present your requests to God,"* (Philippians 4:6-7). The emphasis on "Do not be anxious " didn't stop there, but continued to instruct us not to worry "about anything". Adherence to this instruction is the ONLY way couples can enjoy peace in their marriage. When couples decide to surrender their anxieties and worries to God, he replaces our anxieties with His peace that surpasses all understanding.

Keep your focus on God. By focusing on God's promises rather than our problems, couples can maintain peace in their home. The bible affirms this in the book of Isaiah 26:3: *"You will keep in perfect peace those whose minds are steadfast, because they trust in you".* Even in the midst of storms, couples will remain unmoved because of their faith in God's goodness and His presence.

Meditate on Scriptures together: Scripture passages that speak of God's promises and peace can be a source of serenity and consolation for couples. The practice of gratitude helps us change our perspective from what we're lacking to what He has already provided. Couples can do this by giving thanks to God for His blessings and the little successes they have achieved in their marriage.

Create a calm environment. Couples should effectively focus their thoughts on God by spending time in a peaceful arena such as a park or a special place at home.

3. Hope: Expecting the Goodness of God

Hope is the conviction that, despite the challenges of the present, God has good things planned for the future. Biblically, hope is a confident anticipation based on God's faithfulness and promises, not a mere wish. That is why the scriptures guarantee the dependability of God's promises thereby encouraging us to have faith in God's unwavering promises.

Have faith in God's unwavering promises. The scripture guarantees the dependability of God's promises. Christians couples are urged to *"hold unswervingly to the hope we profess, for he who promised is faithful"* in Hebrews 10:23. Knowing that God is constant gives us the strength to keep our hope alive even though waiting for restoration may seem like an endless journey.

There's hope for life eternal. We are reminded in Romans 8:18 that *"the glory that will be revealed in us is not worth comparing with our present sufferings."* We have the promise of eternal life, where all restoration will be ultimately fulfilled, notwithstanding how agonizing the wait may be. Looking from the eternal perspective, can help us to become more resilient in enduring temporal trials.

Paul the Apostle explains in 2 Corinthians 12:9 how God's power is made perfect in our weakness. Even when we feel helpless, God's strength keeps us going and gives us faith that He is there and He's working out all things for our good.

Practical Steps to Keep our Hope Alive

Reviewing the Promises of God

Scriptures about God's hope serve as a reminder of His commitment to us, whether we document them or commit them to memory.

You must affirm God's word Daily

By saying out loud or writing down affirmations of God's goodness and promises on a daily basis, our hope is rekindled.

Keeping Hope, Peace, and Faith in our Daily Life

Hope, peace, and faith are all interdependent and sustain one another. Peace keeps us at ease in God's presence, hope points us towards the future He has promised, and faith serves as a reminder of God's dependability. Integrating these attributes into our everyday lives and establishing habits that keep us near to God are essential as we wait for restoration.

Living in the Now While Hoping for the Future

Although hope often guides us toward the future, it's as important to recognize God's presence right now. The scriptures further explain this in clear terms, *"Do not worry about tomorrow, for tomorrow will worry about itself."* Knowing that God is taking care of our future allows us to trust Him completely and liberate ourselves from needless worries by concentrating on the here and now. If I ask, what do you have to lose by trusting God? Absolutely nothing!

Prevent Discouragement

The scriptures in Galatians 6:9 urges us to persevere through the unpleasant and protracted process of waiting: *"Let us not become weary in doing good, for at the proper time we will reap a harvest if we do not give up."* We must remember that God is dependable while we wait and keep our hearts safe from discouragement.

Supporting Each Other

We are admonished to *"encourage one another and build each other up"* in 1 Thessalonians 5:11. During waiting seasons, community support may be quite helpful. Having others who share our faith, whether they be close friends, small groups, or prayer partners, will motivate us to keep going.

I'll share with you examples of heroes of faith in the scriptures that have maintained their faith, peace and hope while waiting for God's restoration. Their testimonies will boost your faith to press on despite all odds, cause the end thereof is glorious.

Scripture Examples: Putting Your Trust in God During Waiting Times

There are numerous accounts of individuals who had to wait for God's restoration can be found throughout the Bible. These examples are meant to inspire and instruct us on the way to go.

Abraham and Sarah

Decades passed before the promise of a child came to pass in the case of Abraham and Sarah. According to Genesis 21:1, "The Lord was gracious to Sarah as he had said, and the Lord did for Sarah what he had promised." Their experience shows us that while God's timetable often differs from ours, we can always depend on His unfailing promises.

Joseph

Before the status of Joseph was elevated in Egypt, he had to endure treachery, slavery and imprisonment. He remained faithful even in the face of adversity, and ultimately God turned his trials for good. The account of Joseph in the Bible serves as a reminder that God's restoration is greater than we could have ever imagined.

David

Despite being anointed, David waited for many years to become king. He endured persecution and adversity throughout this time, yet he trusted God's plan for his life. The virtue of perseverance that David displayed is reflected in Psalm 27:14, *"Wait for the Lord; be strong and take heart and wait for the Lord."* David's testimony teaches us the importance of perseverance and unwavering faith.

Waiting for God's restoration while clinging on to faith, peace, and hope is a path that calls for perseverance, patience, and trust. We can confidently face uncertain times if we firmly ground ourselves in God's nature and promises. Hope provides us the strength to anticipate

God's restoration, peace allows us to rest in His presence, and faith helps us to trust His plan.

The scriptures assure us that God is dependable and will bring about the restoration we want in His own perfect time. We can approach each day with renewed faith, peace and expectation of the blessings He has in store as long as we cling to these principles.

Consistently Trust the Process, even when it seems like nothing is Happening

When everything appears to be stagnant, as a Christian couple, trusting God's process is an act of faith that can strengthen your bond with God and each other. It's difficult to maintain hope when things seem to be the same, but God's timing and purpose are flawless, even when they're out of our line of sight.

However, the good news is that there are several ways couples can consistently trust the process God is taking them through even when it seems like all hope is lost.

Recognize that God Is Sovereign

The foundation of putting our trust in God is acknowledging His sovereignty, or His absolute power and command over all. The sovereign power of God is displayed in the scriptures in Isaiah 55:8-9, God declares, *"For my thoughts are not your thoughts, neither are your ways my ways... As the heavens are higher than the earth, so are my ways higher than your ways and my thoughts than your thoughts.* "The larger picture, which includes aspects we cannot comprehend, is seen by God. The larger picture, which includes aspects we cannot comprehend, is seen by God. As a couple, keep in mind that even when you can't see it, He is actively working behind the scene and is aware of the tiniest details about your life and marriage Because His sovereignty allows you to depend on His knowledge instead of your own, you can therefore take solace in that.

Engaging the Strength of Trust in Tough Times

Trust is essential in any marriage, but it becomes much more crucial when it seems like nothing is changing. Recognizing God's authority over your marriage and all other facets of your life is necessary to trust Him in these times. Trusting God is simple when everything is going smoothly, but true trust is put to the test when things are unclear. The scripture makes it clear to us in *Proverbs 3:5-6,*

"Trust in the Lord with all your heart, and lean not on your own understanding; in all your ways acknowledge Him, and He shall direct your paths."

Couples are expected to fully trust God during times of struggle or stagnation, even if they are unable to comprehend the causes of their current situation. Relying on God's wisdom and direction rather than one's own knowledge or the situation is what it means to trust God.

Couples can support one another putting their trust in God even if they don't get results right away. They can keep in mind that God is forming and sculpting their hearts behind the scene, preventing them from panicking or losing patience. Even when it appears like nothing is happening, they need to remind themselves that God is always dependable.

The Process of Patience: Building Endurance

Christians couples should practice patience, particularly when waiting seems to be taking longer than anticipated. The Bible encourages us to develop one's faith and character which is a gradual process that calls for perseverance and endurance.

"But let patience have its perfect work, that you may be perfect and complete, lacking nothing." (James 1:4)

The book of James highlights that a key element of spiritual maturity is patience. Couples have the chance to develop their character, learn to persevere, and strengthen their faith in God during the waiting periods.

Couples who are waiting together might encourage one another to be patient by changing their thought pattern on how they view the process God is taking them through. They must learn to concentrate on what God is doing in them through the process rather than what is not happening. Even in the absence of instant results, when the virtue of patience is in place couples are empowered to persevere and press on, believing that God is at work. You can actually pray for patience at any time, and God will give it to you.

Maintaining Faith in the Unseen

It is necessary to have confidence in the invisible in order to trust God's process. Faith entails believing in God's promises, even when the results are not immediately apparent. The scriptures above are pointers that will enable us to keep our faith without flinch while we rely on God's promises.

"For we walk by faith, not by sight." (2 Corinthians 5:7)

"Now faith is the substance of things hoped for, the evidence of things not seen." (Hebrews 11:1)

Oftentimes, couples may find it difficult to observe the progress in their marriage or in their individual lives. However, truth be told, faith is the proof that God is still at work even when nothing else seems to be happening. For couples, faith is the conviction that, despite what the outside world may say, God is at work in their lives and in their marriage.

By continually reminding themselves of God's promises, Christian spouses will help each other grow in their faith. Couples can cling to promises about His supply, peace, or capacity for restoration even in the absence of any observable outcomes. They fortify their relationships with God and each other as a result.

The Role Communication and Prayer plays in Trusting God's Process

Prayer is one of the most effective strategies couples may engage to get through periods where nothing seems to be happening. Couples have to communicate their desires, invite God into their problems, and experience His peace through consistent prayers. In addition to facilitating contact with God, prayer breaches communication between Christian spouses.

"Be anxious for nothing, but in everything by prayer and supplication, with thanksgiving, let your requests be made known to God; and the peace of God, which surpasses all understanding, will guard your hearts and minds through Christ Jesus." (Philippians 4:6-7).

Prayer is an act of faith because it recognizes that God is in charge. Prayer enables couples to experience God's peace, which transcends their circumstances, even when nothing seems to change. It is also a way of giving up control and putting your faith in God that He will answer in His own time.

Couples can pray together on a daily basis, bringing their wants and worries to God and believing that He will hear them. Couples who pray together are also able to have an attitude of thankfulness and recognize that God is at work even when it does look like it.

Acquiring the Ability to Rest in God's Authority

Learning to rest in God's sovereignty is one of the most important lessons to be learned in times of waiting. Even when a couple's effort seems not to yield anything, they must understand that God is in charge. Trusting that God is in control and that He is arranging things in His own way is what it means to rest in Him.

We can be rest assured that the Lord Himself will move mountains for us and fight on our behalf as He promised in (Exodus 14:14):

"The Lord will fight for you; you need only to be still."

Couples are occasionally inclined to act independently, attempting to control circumstances or impose solutions. But God wants us to believe that He is in charge and that we should rest in His authority. Knowing that God is working things out in ways we may not fully comprehend allows couples to find peace when they put their rest in Him.

Couples must imbibe the habit of supporting one another in stepping back and letting God run their marriage. Letting go of worry and accepting the peace that comes from understanding that God is in control is what it means to rest in His God's authority. Couples can have faith that God is at work at all times.

Be Thankful While Waiting

Finally, when it looks like nothing is happening, it is important to develop an attitude of thankfulness. couples can choose to concentrate on what God has done and is doing rather than focusing on what is missing. cultivating an act of gratitude makes it easier for couples to turn their attention from the problems to the promise. No wonder the reason why scriptures instruct us to give thanks even when things aren't going the way we imagine.

"In everything give thanks; for this is the will of God in Christ Jesus for you." (1 Thessalonians 5:18)

Gratitude in any situation, including waiting, turns the attention from uncertainty and annoyance to faith and trust. Even during challenging times, couples' hearts remain receptive to God's grace when they are grateful.

While they wait, couples may take some time to thank God for His faithfulness and count their blessings as the popular hymnal says "Count your blessings and name them one by one. This process will keep couples linked to one another and preserve hope by adopting this thankful attitude.

Trusting God's method is not always simple as people often talk about it nowadays, particularly when it appears like nothing is happening. However, for Christian couples, it is a crucial aspect of their marriage and spiritual journey. Couples may face even the most trying times with hope and assurance if they recognize God's perfect timing, exercise patience, cling to their faith, pray together, trust in His sovereignty, and cultivate the attitude of thankfulness.

Christian couples must keep in mind that God is constantly at work in the background, even when it seems like nothing is happening, as they navigate these difficult times. His intentions for their union are good, and they can have faith that His method will lead them to excel in their marriage and model younger generation, singles and soon to wed youths that God is still in the business of making their marriage only when they consistently trust and follow His process even when it seems like nothing is working.

- **God's Faithfulness in Restoration.**

Our God is a God restoration. The concept of restoration has been present since the inception of the world documented in the scriptures since the beginning of time, resembling a golden thread. God's faithfulness in restoration, whether it is the restoration of creation after the fall of man, rebuilding of Israel after exile, or the mending of damaged marriages, is both a promise and a reality that gives hope to the lost, the broken, and the wounded.

Restoring what has been lost or damaged is at the core of God's redemptive purpose. Both Christian and non-Christian couples who are facing challenges, separation, or even the possibility of divorce will find hope in this divine fidelity. Human limits and failings do not restrict God's ability to rebuild marriages, and His constancy is always available to those who seek His involvement.

Both Christian and non-Christian marriages can experience times of discord, betrayal, intimacy loss, and emotional detachment over time. Marriages are restored, demonstrating God's faithfulness throughout these trying times. With an emphasis on marriage restoration, this chapter will examine God's faithfulness in restoration of Christian and non-Christian marriages by drawing out biblical promises, instances, and precepts that demonstrate His redeeming and restorative character.

The Character of God Faithfulness

Throughout Scripture, one of God's primary attributes is the concept of faithfulness. God's faithfulness is unqualified, unflinching, and unchangeable. His faithfulness is founded on His character rather than our deeds. Paul tells us in 2 Timothy 2:13 that *"He remains faithful, because He cannot deny Himself, even if we are unfaithful."* God's faithfulness is assured because it is based on His immutability rather than our own merit.

God's covenant with His people is closely linked to his faithfulness; in Deuteronomy 7:9, we are reminded to,

"Know therefore that the Lord your God is God, the faithful God who keeps covenant and steadfast love with those who love Him and keep His commandments, to a thousand generations."

God's faithfulness is linked to His covenantal promises, and He will always fulfill His word, even when His people fail to put their trust in Him. This will take us to vividly examine God's restoration in creation so we can have a better understanding of God's faithfulness in restoration.

God's Restoration of Creation: A Divine Pattern

The creation story is the first example of restoration in the Bible. In Genesis 1, God creates the heavens, the earth, and everything within them, saying that it is "very good"

(Genesis 1:31). However, the perfection of creation was tainted when sin entered the earth as a result of Adam and Eve's Disobedience to God's instruction. The entire order of creation was affected by the effects of sin, not just humans. God's purpose of restoration was initiated even in the midst of brokenness.

God promises a Savior in Genesis 3:15, who will vanquish the serpent and mend the rift between God and humanity. The promise of a Redeemer who would mend everything that sin has destroyed is revealed in this first sight of the gospel. This promise of restoration appears again throughout the Old Testament in many ways, leading up to the arrival of Jesus Christ, who completes God's plan of redemption and restoration, Hallelujah.

Restoration through Jesus Christ

Jesus Christ is the pinnacle of God's deed of restoration. God restores the bond between humans and Himself, which was destroyed by sin, through the death and resurrection of Jesus Christ, His only begotten son. This divine design was revealed to us in Colossians 1:19–20:

"For God was pleased to have all his fullness dwell in him, and through him to reconcile to himself all things, whether things on earth or things in heaven, by making peace through his blood, shed on the cross."

God has paved the road for our complete restoration to Him by Christ Jesus. Forgiveness is only one aspect of this restoration process; it also aims to change us from the inside out, revitalize our hearts, and give us a new meaning, which the scriptures assure us about in Romans 8:1

"There is now no condemnation for those who are in Christ Jesus." Through Jesus, God restores our identity, offering us freedom from guilt and shame.

Restoration of Marriage: Sacred Covenant

Another instance where God's commitment to restore is seen is in marriage, as seen in Genesis 2:24:

"Therefore, a man shall leave his father and mother and be joined to his wife, and they shall become one flesh, "laying the groundwork for marriage. The intimate, devoted, and unbreakable bond between God and His people is what this union is supposed to represent.

However, conflicts, betrayals, separations, and even divorces occur in marriages as a result of sin and human frailty. Hence, the institution of marriage has not been abandoned by God in His boundless love. Even the most damaged marriages can be restored and revitalized by his faithfulness to restore. God promises to restore the "one flesh" union that marriage symbolizes in the midst of marital problems.

God's Faithfulness in Restoring Christian Marriages

God's faithfulness in restoring Christian marriages can be better understood in the above key principles I'll be sharing with you:

Covenantal Faithfulness

Just as God keeps His promises, He expects spouses to keep their commitments to one another. God wants a spouse who is as committed to their marriage as He is, one who stays together through tough times.

Redemption and Restoration

God is described in the scripture as a God who restores what is broken. Whether it is a marriage, friendship, or a heart, God is still in the business of redeeming people. He restores hope, heals wounds and wounded hearts.

Unconditional Love

God's love is unconditional, and He expects married spouses to love one another with the same fervor and dedication. God's love endures despite couples failing one another, He still offers forgiveness and the chance for reconciliation.

Mercy and Grace

199

Marriage is a partnership of two imperfect individuals coming together. The ability to overcome flaws, weaknesses, and failings is provided by God's grace. Even after times of grief or betrayal, couples can find restoration because of His kindness toward people who turn from their sins.

The Role of God in Restoring Christian Marriages

Restoring a Christian couple's marriage is directly related to their relationship with God. The foundation of our faith offers the structure for restoration when challenges emerge, as a result of infidelity, a breakdown in communication, or distance emotionally. Christian marriage is about two individuals and their relationship with Christ, not just about two people. When a marriage is having problems, the couple is supposed to pray together, seek God's direction, and rely on the Holy Spirit for restoration, knowledge, and strength.

Prayer as a Restoration Tool

Prayer is an effective strategy for restoring a broken or challenged marriage. Couples have to come together to ask God to intervene in their problems stand seek His will for their marriage through prayer. Prayer also gives couples a way to reflect on themselves, which enables them to look at their attitudes and feelings for each other. Couples give themselves over to God's transformational power when they present Him with their disappointments, uncertainties, and pains.

For instance, when a couple decides to pray together on a regular basis, they start to experience positive changes in their marriage after years of conflict. They experience healing, understanding, and a revitalized feeling of love as a result of prayer, which aligns them with God's intention for their relationship.

God's Will for Restoration

God shows His desire for restoration throughout the Bible, not just for individuals but also for marriages and families. This is revealed in His word in the book of Joel 2:25, God promises us,

"I will restore to you the years that the locust has eaten." This promise reflects God's power to redeem and restore what was lost or broken.

God's ability to repair and redeem what was damaged or lost is reflected in this promise.

Marriages are no exception to this promise. Even in the most difficult circumstances, God longs for restoration and reconciliation. He has the power to repair whether or not a couple believes in Him or not, particularly if they turn to Him for direction and healing.

The Role of Reconciliation and Forgiveness

The ability to forgive is one of the most significant ways that God's faithfulness is displayed in marital restoration. In marriage, there will always be disagreements and hurt. But the secret to restoration is forgiveness. Jesus teaches us about forgiveness in Matthew 18:21–22.

"Then Peter came up and said to Him, 'Lord, how often will my brother sin against me, and I forgive him? As many as seven times?' Jesus said to him, 'I do not say to you seven times, but seventy-seven times."

This implies that forgiveness is an essential asset in the process of restoration of marriages. Couples who desire to enjoy a heaven on earth marriage must develop the attitude of forgiving one another before they can enjoy God's faithfulness in restoring the marriage.

Being Humble and Submitting to the Wisdom of God

Humility, or acknowledging our need for assistance, is frequently the first step toward restoration. The bible states this in James 4:10 *"Humble yourselves before the Lord, and he will lift you up,"*. Humility is crucial for both Christian and non-Christian marriages. We make room for God's power to operate in us and our relationships when we acknowledge our shortcomings.

Submitting to God in a Christian marriage requires spouses to pray for His wisdom and direction in every aspect of their marriage. Christian couples will discover clarity and direction through prayer and reliance on God, particularly during trying times.

Seeking therapy, becoming receptive to understanding one another's needs, and making the decision to listen more intently are examples of humility and submission in non-Christian relationships. God can still operate in their hearts and lead them to decisions that result in healing and restoration even if they don't acknowledge God as their guide.

The Strength of Sacrifice and Love

The ultimate example of selfless love is the love that God has for mankind. This type of love is vital for marital restoration. In 1 Corinthians 13:4–7, Paul explains what love is like.

"Love is patient and kind; love does not envy or boast; it is not arrogant or rude. It does not insist on its own way; it is not irritable or resentful... Love bears all things, believes all things, hopes all things, endures all things."

The Holy Spirit gives Christian spouses the ability to love one another unconditionally, mirroring the selfless love of Christ. They rely on God's power to remain persistent, patient, and optimistic throughout difficult moments in their marriage.

God's teachings of sacrifice and love nevertheless have a strong influence in non-Christian marriages. Couples start to recover when they put one other need ahead of their own and choose to be kind, understanding, and patient with one another. These attributes of love are ingrained in God's nature, whether they are recognized or not, and He is dependable in bestowing blessings onto people who strive to live by them.

Identity and Purpose Restoration in Marriage

When a marriage is struggling, both couples may go through an identity crisis and feel unworthy or inadequate. Reminding each other of their intrinsic value and significance is part of God's restoration work. This is evident in God's word to us in Ephesians 2:10:

"For we are God's handiwork, created in Christ Jesus to do good works, which God prepared in advance for us to do."

In marriage, Christian couples discover and confirm their identity in Christ by consulting God's word. This knowledge gives them a sense of comfort and confidence, which enables them to love each other without reservation. Nevertheless, God gives non-Christian couples their feeling of worth and purpose by reassuring them that they deserve respect and affection. A revitalized feeling of one self-fosters a more positive dynamic and enables the marriage to thrive.

God's Unwavering Faithfulness Despite Human Failings

It is evident when human strength fails that God's faithfulness is most apparent. *"The steadfast love of the Lord never ceases; his mercies never come to an end; they are new every morning; great is your faithfulness,"* indeed God's love is true and pure even when it doesn't look like it (Lamentations 3:22–23). God's faithfulness has the power to uphold and repair a marriage when it experiences severe difficulties.

Christian couples must trust God's faithfulness, especially in the face of seemingly insurmountable challenges. Couples can without doubt trust that He will fulfill His promises because He is able to create a path where none appears to exist. Even in non-Christian marriages, God still remains faithful. Regardless of one's views, he gives mercy and hope to everyone who seeks it and has the power to effect change even when all human efforts have failed.

The Ultimate Aim of Restoration – Reflect the Love of God

In the end, God's involvement in marital restoration demonstrates His desire for everyone to know His grace and love. A reunited marriage is a testament to God's power and mercy, allowing His love to shine through. A marriage that God has repaired, whether it be in a Christian or non-Christian marriage, will reassure and inspire others that marital healing and restoration are possible.

The scripture assures us of His love which is reflected in His willingness to restore our marriage in John 13:34-35,

"A new commandment I give to you, that you love one another: just as I have loved you, you also are to love one another. By this all people will know that you are my disciples, if you have love for one another."

God's love becomes a reflection of His own when He restores your marriage, giving the world a glimpse of who He is.

The Bible is filled with examples of God's constancy in restoration, which demonstrate His willingness to change, heal, and restore. God is unwavering in his resolve to make all things new, whether it means bringing us back to our inner peace, restoring our marriages, reviving our purpose, or giving us hope for ultimate restoration. We witness the fullest manifestation of God's restoration love in Jesus, who offers us a life full of meaning and hope and helps us establish a proper connection with Him.

God's involvement in restoring non-Christian and Christian marriages demonstrates His deep dedication to restoration, love, and togetherness. Through prayer, reconciliation, sacrificial love, forgiveness, and humility, God revives and makes broken or challenged marriages beautiful. His kindness and love transcend all borders; they are not constrained by our flaws or our convictions.

Couples in Christian marriages have the exceptional advantage of depending on God as their pillar, receiving support and direction from Him. God's love, forgiveness, and humility may nevertheless be powerfully restored in non-Christian marriages, proving His love for everyone. In the end, God's constancy endures whether through faith or just a desire for restoration. Every marriage, no matter where it began, is within His loving grasp because He is a God who renews, restores, and redeems.

We can have confidence that God, in His complete faithfulness, will heal us when life breaks or depresses us. Even if we might not always comprehend the time or approach, His commitment is unwavering. Knowing that God will finish the excellent job He has begun in us, we may find strength, peace, and our joy renewed as we rely on His faithfulness (Philippians 1:6).

Chapter 10

Standing For Your Relationship

Have you lost count of how many relationships you've lost in the past? Are you troubled; think you're never going to be able to keep any meaningful relationship? Have you been heartbroken, and you are giving up on starting another relationship? This last chapter will certainly help you as we focus on "Pre-marital Relationships".

Have you found yourself fighting going back and forth with your better half the one that God called you to be with and you're not understanding why this relationship so hard when God put you all together well look here, I am going to tell you why because God puts y'all together and anything that God puts together the enemy hates. So, the enemy is fighting tooth and nail so y'all do not get to the altar because once y'all say I do it's a losing battle now let me make a disclaimer just because God put y'all together does not mean that you aren't going to go through anything but you remember two people are fighting against the enemy oops sorry not two three people fighting against him he's already lost. So, you ask yourself how do I get God to restore my relationship well we all know prayer works and we all know fasting works but you know what you have to have all at the end of the day faith. So where is your faith.

The concept of "standing for your relationship" has become both difficult and very significant. Beyond just staying together, this concept includes a purposeful, intentional choice to foster, safeguard, and grow a relationship in spite of the challenges and difficulties that life always brings. Standing for your relationship requires active commitment, a process that calls for emotional maturity, resilience, compromise, and often a readiness to develop with the other person.

Standing for your relationship is based on the fundamental belief that love alone cannot maintain a relationship, particularly a long-term one. While love and devotion provide a solid foundation, relationships that would last long require communication, affection, and respect for one another, shared objectives, and individual responsibility. Prioritizing these values and continuously deciding to make investments in your partner's welfare and the relationship's stability are necessary to stand for a relationship.

Relationships nowadays take place in a changing cultural environment. Sometimes it is harder to sustain a relationship than it used to be because of social media, shifting gender norms, and a greater focus on personal satisfaction. External influences and pressures, such job responsibilities, technology diversions, and social expectations about what a "perfect" relationship should look like, may have an impact on relationships today. Insecurities, doubts, and even the urge to choose other routes are often heightened by these pressures.

However, to stand for a relationship, is to navigate these influences together, figure out how to help each other through difficulties, trust God for the return of a departed partner and redefine commitment in an ever-changing world which is often unpredictable.

Understanding Premarital Relationships

Premarital relationships are a critical stage in the process of getting married. They provide the soon-to-be-married the chance to get to know one another well, determine compatibility, and establish the groundwork for a long-term commitment. In Christian setting, premarital relationships serve as a prelude to a holy commitment rather than just a way to enjoy company. Couples have the chance to cultivate the traits and knowledge that will enable a happy and healthy marriage by navigating this period with purpose and values.

The Objective of Premarital Relationships

Premarital relationships often serve deeper purposes than it seems. These relationships serve as a period that enables an individual to determine compatibility, faith and life objectives, even though romantic love and attraction inevitably play a big part. Premarital relationships provide an opportunity to create a bond that respects God's plan for marriage, which is based on love, respect, and dedication. In the Christian setting, the scripture also endorses premarital relationships in Genesis 2:24.

"Therefore, a man shall leave his father and mother and hold fast to his wife, and they shall become one flesh,"

This passage of the scripture emphasizes marriage's ultimate goal of unity—a deep union including the heart, intellect, and spirit. Premarital relationships should thus be seen as a time to develop mutual respect, trust, and understanding and should be treated with the respect that comes with marriage because of its significant commitment. The above are the reasons why you must understand and know the importance of engaging in premarital relationship before marriage.

It Establishes a Basis of Honesty and Trust

The foundation of every good relationship is built on honesty and trust. During premarital relationship, couples should be honest with one another about their values, aspirations, strengths, and shortcomings. The scriptures reveal the importance of being honest in premarital relationships liking an honest answer to a "kiss on the lips' in Proverbs 24:26, which indicates that relationship and intimacy are fostered by honesty. Honest couples are able to handle anxieties, and establish limits that make both parties feel respected, safe, and appreciated.

Being dependable and consistent is another aspect of developing trust. Couples create a foundation of security that gets them ready for the more intense commitment of marriage when they behave and speak with honesty. The foundation of emotional safety is trust, which allows both parties to communicate honestly without worrying about criticism and builds a relationship built on acceptance and understanding.

Gaining Knowledge about Conflict Resolution and Compatibility

Being compatible goes beyond simple physical attractiveness; it also entails sharing similar values, beliefs, lifestyle preferences, and future goals. Even while no two people will ever agree on everything, talking about basic issues like their faith, family relationships, finance, and goals for the future helps couples assess their level of alignment in important areas. The scriptures in Amos 3:3 talks about this:

"Do two walk together unless they have agreed to do so?" Couples who agree on important life issues have a common goal, which gives them the courage to pursue marriage.

Learning how to settle disputes amicably and productively is crucial at the premarital stage. There will always be disagreements, but how well a couple handles conflict will influence how well their relationship works out in the long run. In the epistle of Paul to Ephesians 4:26 we're encouraged to manage our anger:

"In your anger do not sin: Do not let the sun go down while you are still angry."

This verse focuses on settling conflicts between couples quickly and with respect, which enables them to develop constructive communication and emotional control habits.

Establishing Limits and Upholding Values

Premarital relationships are also an opportunity to set relational and personal boundaries that respect each person's values. Setting boundaries helps to safeguard the relationship's physical, emotional, and spiritual components while promoting a healthy pace of development. Abstaining from all forms of sexual immorality until marriage is a common example of limits in marriage, which is consistently in line with biblical call for purity in 1 Thessalonians 4:3-4:

"For this is the will of God, your sanctification: that you abstain from sexual immorality; that each one of you know how to control his own body in holiness and honor."

Maintaining individual connections, respecting one another's values, and safeguarding personal time are all included in setting boundaries. Maintaining these limits before marriage helps couples to cultivate self-control and respect that will benefit them in marriage. Respecting limits helps couples build mutual respect and trust, which fosters a relationship that emphasizes both personal development and shared commitment.

Emotional Maturity and Communication

One of the most important qualities a couple may acquire in their premarital relationship is effective communication. Listening, empathy, and understanding are all components of communication that go beyond mere using words. The bible advised us regarding communication to focus on becoming a good listener and points out the importance of patience in James 1:19:

"Everyone should be quick to listen, slow to speak and slow to become angry".

When getting ready for marriage, emotional maturity is another crucial component you must possess. The qualities of maturity include self-awareness, emotional control, and a readiness to accept responsibility for one's deeds. Emotionally mature couples are able to handle difficulties with empathy rather than being impulsive, which creates a secure and caring atmosphere. To be emotionally mature, one must also embrace change, work toward bettering oneself, and support one another's progress.

Growth and Spiritual Alignment

For Christian couples, spiritual alignment is a starting point and a major part of their life while preparing for marriage. Couples that share the same spiritual perception have a common purpose and are guided by the same values and choices. The scripture instructs us sternly to desist from getting involved with unbelievers:

"Do not be unequally yoked with unbelievers".

This emphasizes how crucial it is to surround oneself with those who share one's faith and devotion to God. When both couples have a similar spiritual background, they support one another, pray together, and stand firm in faith to get through tough times.

However, spiritual growth does not imply that partners will always have the same level of faith. The secret is a shared dedication to personal development and the willingness to support one another all along the way. As they progress towards marriage, this shared commitment creates a strong bond and a feeling of togetherness between them that fortifies the relationship.

The Role of Church and Family

In premarital relationships, the individual's closest to a couple—especially their family and church; plays a significant impact. Seeking direction, advice, and assistance from dependable family members, mentors, or religious leaders gives couples access to other external perspectives and knowledge, as seen in the scripture, Proverbs 15:22:

"Plans fail for lack of counsel, but with many advisers they succeed."

Getting advice from others has trodden the path they are about to tread and who care about the couple's welfare goes a long way in helping them deal with the challenges of a premarital relationship by providing them with accountability and insights.

Preparing for a Lifetime Commitment

In the end, premarital relationships should be handled with an eye toward the future, emphasizing the traits that will keep a marriage strong. Humility, compassion, love, and patience are all necessary for a marriage to thrive. 1 Corinthians 13:4–7, describes love as being kind and patient, free from conceit or envy, rejoices in the truth, and endures in all situations. By fostering these traits in their premarital relationship, couples are laying the bedrock for their lifetime commitment to one another and creating a bond that will endure hardships and become stronger over time.

For couples who are serious about marriage, it is essential to approach this stage with a sense of purpose and a desire to forge a solid, lasting relationship. Together with the knowledge they've received from their premarital experiences, this preparation puts them on the right track for a happy and secured marriage built on mutual respect, faith, and values.

Nevertheless, there's a need for you to know the dangers of not undergoing and understanding the premarital relationship. Christian couples may encounter a number of difficulties that can compromise the integrity and quality of their union if they do not have a firm knowledge of premarital relationships prior to marriage. Stay with me as

I briefly unveil the dangers involved when couples fail to understand the importance of premarital relationships.

The following are some of the main risks:

Spiritual Disconnection and Value Misalignment

Couples may have disagreements on issues like church participation or spiritual priorities if they don't talk about their faith, values, and practices during the premarital relationship stage. Spiritual misalignment may result in rifts and unresolved conflict that impede peace and oneness in the marriage.

Ineffective Conflict Resolution and Communication

Before getting married, a couple may find it difficult to resolve conflicts in a positive way if they don't acquire effective communication techniques. Misunderstandings, animosity, and unsolved disputes will become the outcome.

Trust Issues

Without deliberate conversations about openness, responsibility, and truthfulness, couples may not be able to build the trust necessary for a strong marriage. Without realizing how important trust is, couples will always find it difficult to feel safe and honest with one another. Trust takes time and constant work to develop.

Lack of Self-Control

When premarital purity is not understood, couples will disregard physical boundaries, which may result in regret, guilt, or a loss of respect. Without setting limits, couples run the risk of experiencing spiritual and emotional problems in their marriage.

Lack of a common vision for life and goals

When two people have different ideas about what they want to accomplish with their lives after marriage, it may lead to discord. By talking about objectives during the premarital stage, couples will avoid feeling "unequally yoked" and prepare for a united future.

Christian couples who don't understand premarital relationships will experience poor communication, loss of trust, spiritual misalignment, and inadequate boundaries, all of which might endanger the security of their marriage. Couples will better prepare themselves for a robust, satisfying, and God-centered partnership by devoting time and energy to their marital preparation.

Premarital relationships are ultimately a crucial time for preparation. It is an opportunity to respect God's plan for love, unity, marriage and to establish a relationship that is characterized by grace, love, and patience for those who approach it in the Christian way. Couples who prepare carefully are more prepared to get married with resilience, joy, and the ability to support one another through all of life's challenges. Prioritizing these principles and establishing a solid foundation makes premarital interactions a lovely journey that paves way for a solid, long-lasting marriage.

Hinge your Relationship in Christ

Building a solid, wholesome, and satisfying relationship in a Christian marriage requires that the marriage is firmly established in Christ. Even while all relationships have difficulties, a faith-based marriage seeks to show love, commitment, and purpose from a biblical perspective, seeking God's support and direction.

Here, we will explore the fundamental principles and deliberate attitudes that Christian spouses can engage to hinge their relationship in Christ.

Make Prayer a Priority

One effective strategy that helps couples get closer to God and one another is through prayer. It is crucial for couples to schedule time for both individuals and praying together in Christian relationships. When a couple prays together, they are bringing God into their relationship and asking Him to be the cornerstone of their union. Through prayer, couples give thanks, ask for wisdom, and entrust their worries to God.

Couples develop spiritual intimacy—a special and profound kind of connection that deepens their bond—by praying together. The Bible exhorts Christians to *"pray without ceasing"* (1 Thessalonians 5:17), which does not always entail praying nonstop but rather fostering a habit of constant communion with God. Couples that engage in this activity together get closer and let prayer influence their attitudes, thoughts, and behavior towards one another.

Humility and forgiveness are also fostered by daily prayer. A couple develops a compassionate attitude as they confide in God about their needs and shortcomings, realizing that, by God's grace, they are both work in progress. Couples can pray through arguments and difficulties to gain the discernment, endurance, and fortitude to face difficulties with love and grace.

Study the Word Together

The foundation of a Christian's marriage is the Bible, which also acts as a roadmap for couples looking to establish a union in accordance with God's desire. Couples can learn about God's lessons on love, marriage, forgiveness, patience, and other qualities necessary for a successful relationship by studying the Bible together.

Couples discover God's plan for marriage by scheduling time for Bible study. The bible highlights cooperation, loyalty, and togetherness in Genesis 2:24, which describes two people coming together as **"one body"**. Couples get a deeper knowledge of the principles that ought to guide their relationship by reading and considering the scriptures.

Additionally, studying the bible together encourages couples to discuss issues that affect them both individually and collectively. Reading Scripture together facilitates open communication about spiritual development, challenges, and aspirations while also illuminating one another in their journey of faith. By cultivating a relationship based on common values and an idea in addition to love, this technique fosters a spiritual and intellectual bond through which couples can hinge their relationship in Christ.

Have a Spiritual Covering

For Christian couples who want to hinge their relationship on Christ, belonging to a church, that is, a spiritual covering is very essential. The church provides a network of Christians who share similar faith and beliefs. They serve as a pillar of support through their prayers and encouragement to the couple. The scriptures in Hebrews 10:24-25 urges us to

"Stir up one another to love and good works" and to *"not neglect meeting together."*

Not neglecting the gathering of the brethren is fundamental if couples want to hinge their relationship in Christ alone. Couples who regularly attend church and join a group in the church get access to the knowledge and experiences of older couples who have gone and are still navigating the path of relationships and faith.

Church participation also gives room for couples to be properly mentored according to God's pattern as enshrined in the scriptures. It is quite beneficial to learn from seasoned Christian couples who are an embodiment of a Christ-centered marriage. These mentors assist younger couples develop resilience, forgiveness, and patience while sharing their personal experience on the highs and lows of marriage with them. Couples get more intimate as they serve God and others by getting involved in church activities together, whether it be via outreach initiatives or Bible studies.

Seek Godly and Wise Counsel

Every relationship has its share of difficulties, but a Christian couple's dedication to seeking wise counsel is an added advantage we enjoy. Premarital counseling, mentoring, and marital counseling, are all beneficial resources for Christian couples looking to hinge their relationship on God in order to improve and fortify their union.

Whether from a pastor, a Christian counselor, or a married mentor couple, godly advice aids in the development of healthy communication and conflict-resolution techniques. Premarital counseling is especially beneficial because it enables couples to examine fundamental subjects like expectations, money, communication patterns, and family planning from the lens of the scriptures. Regular check-ins with a mentor or counselor will be of tremendous help to married couples who stay in line with God's teachings and get through challenging times.

Adopt Christlike Attributes in a Relationship

Both parties must exhibit Christlike traits in order for their relationship to be hinged on Christ, particularly those attributes listed in Galatians 5:22–23: *love, joy, peace, patience, kindness, goodness, faithfulness, gentleness, and self-control.* Couples foster an environment of compassion, forgiveness, and respect in their relationship by working to cultivate these traits.

The two essential attributes that assist couples in resolving disagreements amicably are patience and humility. Couples that put these traits into practice are able to listen intently, react gently, and steer clear of pointless disputes. Just as Christ's love for mankind was selfless, sacrifice is a part of a Christ-centered relationship.

Put Limits in Place to Honor God

Christian couples who are dedicated to a Christ-centered relationship must practice setting appropriate boundaries. Setting limits protects the relationship from potential pitfalls and helps maintain emotional stability, purity, and respect. The Bible exhorts Christians to respect their bodies, which are the temples of the Holy Spirit, and to abstain from sexual immorality (1 Corinthians 6:19-20).

Limiting physical contact to prevent temptation, establishing explicit guidelines for alone time, and making a commitment to responsibility are some examples of boundaries for dating or engaged couples. Setting and maintaining boundaries helps married couples safeguard their relationship by preventing unsuitable interactions and circumstances that might erode trust. Respecting God and sustaining a relationship based on integrity and respect are the goals of boundaries, not about imposing limitations.

Serving One Another in your Daily Life and Ministry

Serving others is an integral part of a Christ-focused relationship because Christian love naturally leads to service. Throughout His life, Jesus exemplified service, but especially when He washed His disciples' feet, He said in John 13:15:

"I have set you an example that you should do as I have done for you"

Couples who serve together reflect Christ's love in their community and create a feeling of purpose. Serving one another in the relationship by lending a hand with house chores, encouraging one another's goals, or providing consolation are examples of the love and concern that Christ implores couples to exhibit. These acts of kindness create a culture of gratitude, respect, and support.

Support One Another's Spiritual Growth and Call

Both spouses must support one another's own spiritual growth if they want their relationship to be firmly hinged and flourish in Christ. This involves honoring time spent in prayer, Bible study, or in reflection. Being there for one another amid spiritual difficulties and acknowledging one other's faith accomplishments are two ways that we can support one another's spiritual development.

Couples can support one another's vocation, share insights from their own spiritual thoughts, and encourage each other to participate in church activities as ways to assist each other grow in their calling. Couples must also challenge one another to uphold their morals and faith by holding each other responsible and accountable.

Recognizing God's Will for Marriage

Finally, Christian spouses must embrace and comprehend God's purpose for marriage in order to hinge their relationship in Christ. According to the Bible, marriage is a holy institution that symbolizes Christ's love for the Church, Ephesians 5:31–32,

"A man will leave his father and mother and be united to his wife, and the two will become one flesh".

These scriptures highlight that a marriage is a partnership in which both spouses are expected to love one another without conditions, help each other out, and cooperate to further God's kingdom.

Marriage is a covenant, not just a contract that represents God's unending love for His people. Christian couples must come to the realization that their love is meant to serve as a model for other Christian and even non-Christian couples when they acknowledge marriage as a partnership in faith with the intention of glorifying God. Their relationship is strengthened by this goal, which serves as a reminder that their dedication transcends their own satisfaction and is eventually a part of God's redeeming mission in the world.

Resolve Conflicts with the Lens of God's Word

Conflict resolution is an essential ability every guy or lady in a relationship must acquire or possess. For Christian couples, God's Word offers a special basis for handling disputes with love, humility, and wisdom. The Bible provides Christians with guidelines for resolving disputes, promoting peace, and expanding understanding. Through the application of God's Word, couples can transform conflicts into an avenue for personal and collective development, harmony, and reaffirmed dedication.

In this chapter I will be giving you a detailed explanation on how Christian spouses can settle conflicts through the lens of God's word and its benefits.

Understanding Conflict's Contribution to Growth

Conflict is a natural aspect of life, including relationships, according to scriptures. The act of conflict itself is not immoral; it may be a teaching tool and a way to better comprehend one another's perspectives. The scriptures in Proverbs 27:17 corroborates this, *"As iron sharpens iron, so one person sharpens another."* Both spouses stand to benefit from conflict in a marriage by learning, developing, and adapting. Disagreements when handled with love and respect as the potential to highlight areas that need forgiveness, communication, or attention.

God gives room for conflicts to test us, hone our character and bring us closer to Him. This perception motivates couples to approach conflicts with openness, and a desire to strengthen their bond and their faith rather than with fear or being all defensive.

Pray for God's Direction

In every Christian relationship, prayer is essential, but it's more important when there is conflict. Couples must engage in prayer both individually and together before resolving conflicts to ask God for wisdom, patience, and direction. In Philippians 4:6-7, Christians are urged to entrust all of their worries to God, who only can and will protect their hearts and minds with His peace.

Praying before bringing up delicate topics allows God to be included in the discussion and fosters humility. Couples may pray for wisdom, clarity, and the capacity to listen with love. In order to promote empathy and understanding, they should also pray for one another's needs and hurts. Couples who approach conflicts with prayer are less defensive and are reminded that they are working towards fulfilling God's will together.

Embracing Self-Reflection and Humility

Humility is a key element of conflict resolution as it shifts the focus from winning an argument to comprehending and mending the relationship. Christian couples are counseled in James 4:10, "Humble yourselves before the

Lord, and he will lift you up.", this portrays humility as a necessity in the process of resolving conflicts in any relationships. Being humble in the face of disagreement means owning up to one's mistakes and being receptive to criticism. Each individual should ask God to show them how they may have contributed to the problem, rather than only focusing on their partner's flaws.

When Jesus said,

"Why do you look at the speck of sawdust in your brother's eye and pay no attention to the plank in your own eye?"

In Matthew 7:3-5, he was simply emphasizing the need for self-reflection in relationships. This concept serves as a timely reminder to Christian spouses to look at their own hearts and behavior before passing judgment on their spouse

Speak with Love and Respect

Conflict resolution requires courteous and transparent communication. Christians are urged to **"speak the truth in love"** (Ephesians 4:15). This entails using polite words rather than harsh or accusing words when communicating your worries and disappointments. Effective communication entails empathy, active listening, and an emphasis on comprehending one another's points of view rather than just reacting or building a wall of defense around you.

It is often helpful for couples to practice the use of "I" statements rather than "You" statements while they are in the midst of conflict. For instance, one may say, "I feel unheard when we talk about certain issues," as opposed to, "You never listen to me." This strategy lessens culpability and encourages candid discussion.

"A gentle answer turns away wrath, but a harsh word stirs up anger," (Proverbs 15:1)

A safe environment for conversation should be established and escalation avoided with the use of a soft tone and thoughtful choice of words.

Furthermore, listening is an act of love.

"Everyone should be quick to listen, slow to speak, and slow to become angry," (James 1:19)

A settlement including empathy and respect is more likely to be reached when both parties feel heard and understood.

Put Grace and Forgiveness into Practice

A fundamental aspect of the Christian faith, forgiveness is also a crucial element in resolving disputes. According to Colossians 3:13, Christians should

"Bear with each other and forgive one another if any of you has a grievance against someone, forgive as the Lord forgave you."

Conflicts in a marriage might bring back old disappointments or scars. In order to heal and go ahead in love, forgiveness is necessary.

Ignoring the transgression or acting as if it didn't hurt is not what true forgiveness is all about. Rather, it's an intentional choice to let go of bitterness and the want to exact retribution or harbor grudges. It entails exhibiting grace even in difficult situations and imitating Christ's example of forgiveness. Couples keep resentment from growing in their relationship when they let go of their anger. Couples who keep in mind that both spouses are flawed and in need of God's forgiveness are better able to forgive freely, just as Christ did for us.

Pursuing Peace, Not Victory

Reconciliation should be the aim of a quarrel, not "winning" or proving oneself as being right. *"If it is possible, as far as it depends on you, to live at peace with everyone,"*(Romans 12:18), prioritizing the relationship's well-being over one's urge to be correct or personal pride. Finding a solution that respects each spouse and improves the relationship should be the main goal for Christian couples.

The goal of reconciliation is to mend the relationship and bring about peace. Couples can look for areas of agreement and collaborate to come up with solutions that demonstrate love, respect, and understanding rather than getting mired in diametrically opposed opinions. Couples should endeavor to create an environment where restoration is valued above rivalry by putting godly values ahead of their own pride.

Setting Appropriate Boundaries and Timing

Setting and maintaining healthy boundaries is crucial to successful conflict resolution. Leaving a heated argument may sometimes stop hurtful remarks or deeds; the bible affirms this in Proverbs 15:28,

"The heart of the righteous weighs its answers, but the mouth of the wicked gushes evil."

It will be of great help to both parties if they take a moment to relax, pray, and think things through, this will enable them to approach and resolve their conflict with clear thought.

Determining when to bring up delicate subjects is another aspect of setting boundaries. According to Ecclesiastes 3:1, *"there is a time for everything."* Conversations that are more courteous and effective are those that result from scheduling specific time to discuss issues in a quiet and private environment.

Setting boundaries also include honoring one another's demand for privacy during moments of tensions. In addition to preventing escalation, allowing each other space to process their feelings also helps both partners approach the conversation with more clarity.

Maintaining an Attitude of Appreciation and Gratitude

In times of disagreement, it's simple to concentrate just on the issue and overlook the positive aspects of the relationship. Nonetheless, maintaining an attitude of appreciation helps in putting disputes in perspective. Christians are urged to *"give thanks in all circumstances"* in 1 Thessalonians 5:18. Couples reduce the severity of conflicts and promote a respectful and peaceful atmosphere by making the decision to value each other's good contributions, strengths, and abilities.

Even in difficult times, a little gesture of gratitude will serve as a reminder of the love that drew a pair together. By being thankful, both spouses appreciate one another, value and keep their commitment to each other.

Recognizing the Process of Growth and Reconciliation

Resolving conflicts is not usually a one-time fix. It is an ongoing process of development, learning and consistent practice. Christians are urged to *"forget what is behind and strain toward what is ahead"* in Philippians 3:13–14. Every disagreement that is settled should be seen by a couple as an opportunity to get closer, communicate better, and develop trust and love together.

Reconciliation lays the foundation for resilience and trust; hence, it often calls for constant work. Couples can improve their relationship and become closer over time by addressing each conflict with openness to growing, learning, and deepening the bond they shared over time.

When we consider conflict from the perspective of God's Word, Christian spouses will handle it with grace and trust. Couples will transform disagreements into learning experiences by putting prayer first, accepting humility, forgiving one another, and focusing on reconciliation rather than winning. Christian couples may resolve conflicts in a manner that benefits their relationship, exalts God, and enhances their spiritual ties if they are dedicated to love, respect, and understanding.

The Place of Mutual Respect

Respect for one another is the cornerstone of a successful marriage because it promotes emotional intimacy, resiliency and understanding. In a marriage where respect is continuously fostered, both parties feel appreciated, encouraged, and empowered to grow together as a couple and as individuals. Respect in marriage goes beyond the absence of disputes; it is an active process of appreciating each other's uniqueness, weaknesses and strength. From a spiritual and psychological perspective, respect for one another helps couples creates a life that is peaceful, harmonious, and purposeful.

The Place of Mutual Respect in Christian Relationships

Mutual respect is a **MUST** in all forms of relationships with Christians or non-Christians. I will share with you the place of mutual respect in Christian relationships, so that we can know the importance of respect in dealing with relationships and to be able to stay clear of anything that can hinder the peace in our relationships as well as marriages. The above are the roles mutual respect plays in Christian marriages.

Biblical teachings on mutual respect have a strong impact on Christian marriage. The sacredness of marriage is emphasized in the Bible, which describes it as a relationship that reflects the bond between Christ and the Church. Scriptures teaches that love and respect should be reciprocated, in Ephesians 5:21–33, couples are implored to submit to one another and show respect.

Biblical Basis for Respect

The bedrock of a Christian marriage is found in Ephesians 5:33, commands women to respect their husbands and husbands to love them. This dual command emphasizes that a happy marriage requires both love and respect. In this sense, mutual respect does not indicate a hierarchy but rather an equal-value, dynamic in which one spouse respects and encourages the other's contributions and position in the marriage.

Roles and Responsibilities

The Christian doctrine often places strong emphasis on the duties and responsibilities that spouses and couples must fulfill. Mutual respect, on the other hand, requires couples to learn to turn these responsibilities from simple duties into displays of affection and gratitude. For instance, a spouse who respects his wife treats her as an equal partner, honors her contributions, and encourages her to pursue her goals and vice versa.

Understanding and Forgiveness

The place of mutual respect in Christian marriages fosters forgiveness and understanding between couples. Respecting one's spouse helps you accept their imperfections and show them love, fostering an environment in which both couples can develop and change together.

Growing Together Spiritually

It creates an atmosphere where spouses grow together spiritually and grow in faith gaining a deeper knowledge of God. An intimate relationship is built when couples respect one another's path and support one another spiritually. Christian couples build a relationship based on the same values and beliefs by praying, worshiping, and studying the Bible together resulting in a much-fulfilled marriage.

The Place of Respect in a Non-Christian Marriage

Mutual respect often stems from many ethical frameworks, societal principles, and cultural values in non-Christian marriages and relationships. Although the strategy put in place may be different: relationships based on mutual respect in the secular world are more balanced, harmonious and fulfilled.

Respecting One Another's Individuality

In non-Christian settings, respect for one another is often based on individual liberty and an understanding of one another's uniqueness. Respect in this context is giving each partner the freedom to voice their thoughts, work for their objectives, and preserve their individuality within the relationship. By valuing each person's individuality, each partner is encouraged to give their All to the relationship and reliance is avoided.

Effective communication and conflict resolution

Effective communication and conflict resolution are essential to mutual respect in non-Christian relationships. Couples who communicate openly, honestly, and respectfully are better able to comprehend one another's needs and emotions. Couples can resolve disagreements without animosity or disdain when they have polite conversations. To be respectful in this situation, one must actively listen, refrain from passing judgment, and collaborate to create solutions that respect both perspectives.

Partnership and Equality

In many non-Christian marriages, the partners are given equal rights to make decisions and share duties, enabling them to make equal contributions in the marriage. Appreciation is strengthened by this egalitarian strategy as both spouses appreciate and recognize one another's opinions and preferences. For instance, choices about money, careers, and family planning are often made jointly, with each partner's opinion recognized and cherished.

Why Mutual Respect Is Essential in Marriage?

Marriage requires mutual respect for a number of reasons.

Emotional Security

When couples treat one another with respect, they provide a secure environment where both partners feel appreciated and safe. This emotional safety promotes a strong bond and trust by enabling everyone to express themselves freely.

Constructive Communication

Appropriate communication avoids miscommunications and needless disputes. Partners may communicate their needs, wants, and worries without worrying about criticism or rejection when they both talk and listen with respect.

Unity in Decision-Making

A respectful marriage fosters the spirit of cooperation. By avoiding power battles and promoting unity in their marriage, couples that subscribe to being mutually respectful make choices that are of great benefits to both parties.

It Impacts the Children Positively

A marriage built on mutual respect serves as an example of good relationship dynamics for couples who have children. Youngsters acquire important lessons about love, compassion, and cooperation by seeing how their parents interact and treat one another. Seeing these teachings will consciously or unconsciously rub off on them, hence, they begin to apply the same model to their own relationships.

Practical Ways to Display Mutual respect in Marriage

Engage in Active Listening

Giving your partner your undivided attention while entirely attempting to comprehend their thoughts and emotions is known as active listening. This kind of listening requires patience, empathy, and an open mind in addition to just hearing what is being said. By demonstrating your appreciation for your spouse's perspectives, active listening fosters an environment where they feel valued and listened to.

Respect One Another's Views and Opinions

Mutual respect requires that you accept your spouse's point of view, even when it appears to be different from yours. This may include acknowledging their emotions, allowing for candid conversations regarding opposing views, and taking their opinions into consideration when taking and making choices.

Be kind and Avoid the Use of Hurtful Words.

The degree of respect in a relationship is greatly impacted by the language that couples speak with one another. While expressions of thanks and support show respect and build confidence, unpleasant comments may damage self-worth and erode trust. Thoughtful, caring communication demonstrates respect and care even when individuals disagree.

Honor Boundaries and Personal Space

In a successful marriage, each partner acknowledges and respects the other's need for leisure and privacy. Whether through self-care, interacting with friends, or engaging in hobbies, respecting boundaries encourages uniqueness and builds marital trust.

Challenges in Upholding Mutual Respect

In a marriage, maintaining mutual respect takes constant work and may be hampered by the following:

Stress and Life Pressures

A marriage can be strained by health problems, financial hardships, or family obligations, which may result in an inadvertent disdain for one partner's needs or emotions.

Communication Style Differences

Misunderstandings may arise from the ways in which each partner communicates with themselves. Instead of resolving disputes, these communication gaps may intensify them if they are not respected.

Unsolved Hurts

It might be challenging to maintain mutual respect if there are unresolved animosities or disputes from the past. In these situations, recovery will require purposeful reconciliation or therapy.

Power Struggles

When one spouse controls the decision-making process or ignores the other's opinions, respect may erode and emotions of imbalance and anger may set in as a result.

Mutual respect is essential in marriage because it forms the basis of a happy, long-lasting, and healthy relationship. Marriage that is rooted in mutual respect not only benefits the couple but also their families and communities because it fosters emotional safety, clear communication, and togetherness.

Restoring Broken Relationships

Human life relies heavily on relationships. Relationships influence how one thinks about one's self, community, and purpose are shaped by interactions, whether they are friendships, familial ties, marital relationships, or professional connections. Even though relationships are essential to our existence, they are also naturally delicate. Relationships may become broken, sometimes apparently irreparably, as a result of miscommunications, betrayals, neglect, or unsolved disputes. Restoring damaged relationships is a very emotional but very fulfilling process that calls for patience, tolerance, dialogues, and readiness to change.

This chapter explores the nature of damaged relationships, the causes of their harm, and the methods and resources available for restoring such relationships.

Human relationships are dynamic and intricate in nature. They are impacted by individual expectations, communication techniques, cultural conventions, and personal experiences. Relationships are often vulnerable to miscommunications and arguments as a result of these interactions.

Why do Relationships End?

Lack of Communication

Assumptions and misconceptions may end a relationship as a result of poor communication between the parties involved. When people don't communicate their ideas, emotions, or worries, little problems might escalate as a result.

Breach of Trust

All relationships are built on trust. Lying, cheating, or divulging confidential information are examples of actions that can permanently break trust and leave one or both parties feeling exposed or deceived.

Unresolved Conflicts

When conflicts or disagreements are not settled appropriately, it may lead to a vicious cycle of animosity. These unsolved problems have the potential to worsen the relationship and may subsequently lead to separation over time.

Abandonment

Maintaining a relationship takes work and care. A person may feel underappreciated or irrelevant if their basic emotional, physical, or even communication requirements are neglected.

External Stress

Relationships may experience excessive stress owing to personal crises, professional demands, or financial needs, which may exacerbate preexisting fractures.

Disparities in Goals or Values

People change throughout time. A relationship may be strained if two people hold different ideals or develop in different directions.

The first step to restoring relationships is to recognize the causes of a broken relationship. Meaningful conversation may be facilitated by reflection and admitting mistakes by both parties.

The Effects of Broken Relationships on our Emotions

In addition to the individuals directly involved, those in their social circles also frequently experience a flood of unpleasant feelings when a relationship is broken or dissolved. It is normal to feel pain, guilt, wrath, and despair. These feelings can, however, act as stimulants for development and change provided, they are well controlled.

Bereavement: Breaking up or ending a relationship can be like losing a loved one. In addition to the individual, people may mourn for the potentials, dreams, and shared experiences that were lost.

Doubting one's Self: A person may start to doubt or even question their involvement or role in the break-up, their value, or their capacity to sustain meaningful relationships.

Anger and Resentment: Resentment and anger are feelings that might result from unfulfilled expectations or from feeling mistreated.

Isolation: Feelings of loneliness can result from broken relationships, particularly if the relationship takes a vital component of one's support system.

It is essential to recognize and deal with these emotions in order to prevent them from impeding the restoration process or bringing emotional baggage into subsequent relationships.

How to Mend Broken Relationship

The process of restoration is slow because it didn't just happen in a flash. The relationship starts tearing apart gradually without any of the parties taking heed to prevent it from being dissolved. Hence, in the process of restoration, both parties must be willing to exercise patience, voluntarily participate and prioritize healing over shifting blame. The essential stages are as follows:

1. *Engage in Self-Reflection*

Spend some time analyzing your own emotions, motives, and behavior before trying to mend a relationship. Couples might have to give answers to the following questions:

- What led to the break-up? Did any particular words, deeds, or occurrences cause the rift?

- What part did you play? It's critical to assume personal accountability for any errors or blunders.

- What do you want to accomplish? Make it clear if you want to make amends for personal closure or for the sake of both parties healing.

2. *Reach Out to Others*

Being sincere and self-awareness are fundamental to the restoration process of any relationship and are developed by self-reflection. Vulnerability is necessary when reaching out to someone following fallout. Start by establishing a conversation:

- ***Select the appropriate medium:*** Genuine conversation can be sparked by a sincere letter, phone call, or discussion in-person.

- ***Recognize the past:*** Describe the nature of the gap honestly and without placing blame on any one.

- ***Declare your intention to make amends:*** To express your intentions and feelings, use "I" sentences. For instance, "I miss our friendship and I regret how things ended."

This gesture establishes the context for further conversation.

3. *Express Yourself Honestly and Openly*

Open communication is essential to restoring understanding and confidence in a relationship. It is safe for both parties to voice their opinions without worrying about criticism or reprisal.

- Engage in active listening by focusing on body language and emotions in addition to words. Rephrase or affirm the other person's sentiments to demonstrate empathy.

- ***Be truthful:*** Trust is fostered by transparency. Acknowledge your errors and explain how you intend to prevent them from happening again.

- ***Avoid Shifting Blame***: Rather of repeating previous wrongs, concentrate on "we" words and cooperative solutions.

4. *Rebuild Trust*

Rebuilding trust is a necessary step in restoring a broken relationship, which requires patience and persistent work:

- ***Follow through:*** To show you're trustworthy, stick to your agreements always

- ***Demonstrate empathy:*** By recognizing and validating the other person's pain.

- Rebuilding trust takes time, so exercise patience. Give the other person space and time they need.

5. *Letting Go and Forgive*

Forgiveness is about letting go of grudges, not about accepting wrongdoing:

- ***Forgive yourself:*** Self-forgiveness is crucial for personal development, even if you were a contributing factor in the break-up.

- Forgiving someone does not imply forgetting the past; rather, it means refusing to allow it to dictate how you engage with them in the future.

- ***Pay Attention to the Future:*** Instead of focusing on previous transgressions, embrace the possibility of a new relationship.

6. *Establish Appropriate Limits*

Both parties will feel appreciated and understood when there are healthy boundaries:

- ***Talk about Needs:*** Clearly state what you both want from the current and future relationship.

- ***Set Boundaries:*** Decide which acts are acceptable and those that are not.

- ***Honor differences:*** Give room for uniqueness while fostering the bond.

7. *Seek help from Professional where Necessary*

Occasionally, the distance between the two people may be too great or the feelings too intense for them to handle on their own. Professional, unbiased advice can be obtained from mentors, counselors, or therapists:

- Family therapy is the best option for mending family ties.

- ***Couples therapy:*** Beneficial for love relationships that are having serious problems.

- ***Experts in conflict resolution:*** Useful in resolving conflicts in the community or at work.

The role of time and patience in restoring broken relationships cannot be overemphasized. Time indeed has the ability to heal. It gives room for feelings to subside and perspective to change. Both parties can concentrate on reflection and personal development during this time. Patience is the key, as hurrying the process can thwart genuine restoration.

However, there are many stories of relationships being restored. After years of silence, a relationship from childhood was restored. Following their survival of infidelity, a couple renews their vows. After years of separation, a parent and child reunite. These stories demonstrate the transformational potential of empathy, forgiveness, and hard work.

The satisfaction of repairing a broken relationship frequently surpasses the suffering experienced during its dissolution. It deepens the tie and cultivates a greater respect for the connection.

Nevertheless, you'll agree with me that not every relationship can or ought to be restored. It could be better to end a relationship if it is abusive, poisonous, or one-sided. In these situations:

- ***Seek Closure:*** To provide both parties clarity, explain your reasons for moving on, if at all feasible.

- Focus on healing by taking care of yourself and surrounding yourself with encouraging individuals.

- ***Embrace new Beginnings:*** Making room for healthy, fresh relationships may be achieved via letting go.

It takes compassion and bravery to mend broken relationships. It calls for vulnerability, self-awareness, and a steadfast dedication to personal development. Even while the path could be difficult, the end result—a restored bond—is priceless.

The process itself is transforming, regardless of whether the restoration results in a bittersweet resolution or brings you closer than ever. In addition to mending the relationship, choosing reconciliation over animosity also benefits your personal emotions and spiritual health.

Broken relationships are, after all, because they may be chances to rewrite your story, not its end.

Prayer for my Relationship

Our Father in heaven,

We are thankful for the gift of love and relationships You have put in place for us, take all the praise in Jesus' name. As we stand together in our relationship, Lord, we pray for Your courage and wisdom. Teach us to communicate with love and truth, to listen with open hearts, and to be patient with one another. As You have offered us grace, grant us the ability to love unconditionally and to forgive swiftly.

Father, shield our relationship from conflict, and other influences. Give us the fortitude to tackle conflicts head-on and the intelligence to resolve them. Help us to respect one another, acknowledge one another's accomplishments, and encourage one another's aspirations.

Above all, help us to keep You at the center of our relationship. Let Your love serves as our cornerstone so that we can firmly stand together in faith, trust, and unity, this we ask in Jesus' name, Amen!

Conclusion

⸺⸻◯⸻⸺

Restoring a broken marriage is tough, but it can happen with faith, honesty, and a real desire to let God lead the way. This path requires trusting God, looking inward, and being willing to work on yourself, even if your marriage didn't start with God at the center. Restoration is possible, but it calls for spiritual growth, personal change, and taking responsibility for your actions in the relationship.

This journey, as explained in this book, requires dedication, faith, and a constant focus on God. It's a process that involves looking within, growing spiritually, and holding tight to God's promises, even when things seem hopeless. The book shares core principles and practical steps for navigating the challenges of a troubled marriage, relying fully on God's wisdom and strength.

The first step is to identify the foundation of your marriage and invite God into it. Even if God wasn't a part of your marriage from the start, He can help you rebuild, but it begins with sincere surrender and recognizing His power.

Restoration can be tough even in God-centered relationships, so it's essential to consider God's design for marriage and to seek His guidance to heal and rebuild.

Doubts will come, but, as the Bible says in James 1:6-7, our faith must stay strong. Faith is the foundation, and each step forward requires trusting God, even when you can't see change right away. There will be lies, pain, and fear trying to hold you back, but focusing on God, His promises, and His power to restore is key. To succeed, you need to hold firm to God's promises despite challenges or silence.

Another important step is self-reflection. To move forward, you need to examine yourself, admit your flaws, and ask for God's help. No one spouse is solely responsible for a broken marriage; both partners play a role. For true growth, it's necessary to own your part and allow God to show you where you can improve. Humility and a willingness to change are the first steps to healing, and as you work on yourself, God can transform you into the spouse He meant you to be.

Prayer and fasting are powerful tools that can strengthen your faith and prepare you for restoration. These practices help you focus on God's plan, seek His guidance, and face the spiritual struggles against your marriage. By spending time in sincere prayer and fasting, you're giving your hopes, fears, and doubts to the One who can heal and restore.

Staying positive is also vital in this journey. Negative thoughts and influences can bring you down and stall your growth. Keeping a hopeful heart, praying for your marriage, and surrounding yourself with supportive people can help you stay focused on God's promises. Avoiding harmful influences and staying active with positive pursuits, like helping others or enjoying hobbies, can keep your mind strong and faithful.

Let the Bible guide you in this process. God's Word offers guidance, comfort, and reassurance of His faithfulness. Regularly reading and applying scripture to your marriage strengthens your faith and aligns your prayers with His plan. Declaring God's promises and asking for His healing power invites His presence into your marriage.

Standing for your marriage is a journey of faith, self-discovery, and growth. Whether God is new in your marriage or has been there from the beginning, the steps outlined in this book can help you get back on track. Stay close to God, trust Him in the process, and believe that He can restore your marriage in His timing.

Most importantly, let your story inspire others. By trusting God through this difficult time, you can encourage others to have faith in their own struggles. You will find peace in knowing that you've let God lead, regardless of how your story unfolds. Keep praying, keep believing, and above all, keep trusting in God.

www.ingramcontent.com/pod-product-compliance
Lightning Source LLC
Chambersburg PA
CBHW061130160726

48006CB00036B/1494